LUCKY
COUNTRY
Confessions of a Vagabond Cellarhand

DARREN DELMORE

HELLMORE PRESS

San Luis Obispo, CA 93401
© 2018 by Darren Delmore
All rights reserved

Library of Congress Cataloging-in-Publication Data is available.

ISBN-978-0-692-18728-9

Book Design by Kenny Boyer

www.darrendelmore.com

Printed in the United States
Digit on the right indicates the number of this printing.
10 9 8 7 6 5 4 3 2 1

LUCKY COUNTRY

Confessions of a Vagabond Cellarhand

"There's no prettier sight than looking back
at a town you've left behind."

—Townes Van Zandt, *I'll Be Here in the Morning*

AUTHOR'S NOTE

Lucky Country: Confessions of a Vagabond Cellarhand is a work of non-fiction and therefore a product of my own self-medicated memory. Out of respect, most names and identifying details have been changed.

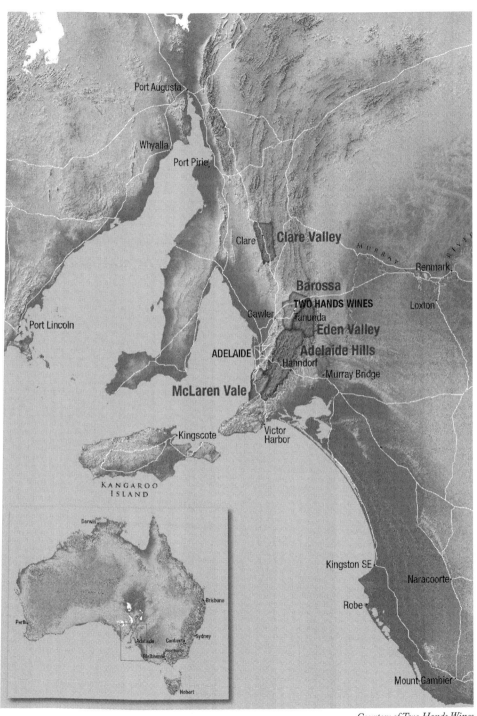

Courtesy of Two Hands Wines

CHAPTER 1

I was broke and bartending at the roughest steakhouse in Humboldt County when it happened. An ultra-unfiltered bottle of 1998 Penfolds Kalimna Bin 28 Shiraz came my way, sparking a fantasy of leaving everything in America by the wayside and working a wine harvest in South Australia and learning how to make the syrupy substance. It would only take me a decade to get there.

Big black Barossa Valley Shiraz, known as Syrah everywhere else but Australia, was nothing like the domestic version of the grape variety that I'd tasted up to that date, nor its homeland's version in France that I'd been fortunate enough to try. The Kalimna was like drinking an iron-enriched, peppered, blackberry smoothie, with a viscosity able to pump one's arteries clean. More importantly, it was powerful enough to temporarily transport me from my somewhat aimless place in the world and ignite my imagination, which is something I'd later learn that high quality wine could do. Shortly after that minor epiphany in 2001, when a splurge for a bottle was $14, I stumbled on the liquidation of some great down under juice at a Grocery Outlet in Eureka, California. The police were in the lot of this discount store every time I visited, and they certainly weren't shopping. One of the cooks at the steakhouse referred to Grocery Outlet as "the dented can food store," which was about right. Marked down bottles of McLaren Vale Cabernet and Shiraz enlivened my most economically impoverished era to date, and gave me nightly hope in the future. I was newly married to a beautiful but violent and jealous girl and living in an over drafted world of one bad career choice after another. Lo and behold, I found case stacked wines from Australia at Grocery Outlet marked down to a third of their value, with older vintages, strange sub-regions and wineries I'd never heard of. Almost all of it was better than anything I previously could afford from California.

These Australian wines spawned a ritual of cooking a steak on the back deck after work around midnight, still dressed in my bartending gear, and washing it down with rich red wine. A midnight ramble, if you will. I'd often hear deer or bears lurking their way toward me through the blackberry vines below, once the garlic, pepper and thyme oil started sending savory signals to the stars. The Cabernet Sauvignon from Tapestry in McLaren Vale paired well with such mountain fare, with its sediment stained bottle. Their Shiraz was impressive too, more zesty and wild with blueberries abounding. I even lucked into a few bottles of decade old D'Arenberg Ironstone Pressings which were concentrated, full of flavor, and lusciously smooth. To find a California wine like any of them would cost upwards of $30 a bottle or more. I returned and bought close to a case of that Tapestry Cab until it was gone, and nabbed every odd Australian higher end wine that fell through the commercial trapdoor into the land full of cereals and frozen pizzas you'd never heard of.

Having dreamed of taking a surf trip to Australia since I was a young teenager, the additional winemaking fantasy made total sense. There was an interference at the time though: actual currency to do it. Aside from serving vodka gimlets and prime rib plates to fishermen, lumberjacks and rapists four nights a week, my then wife and I were truly broke and existing check to check. On the bright side, I had just finished my very first wine harvest experience at a tiny winery called Whitethorn, and I was hooked. I was able to see the mystery of how wine is made on a very high end, micro-production level, and though I didn't know what notes the winemaker was jotting down in her notepad, her codes on her French oak barrels, or the amount of yeast and things she measured out for her fermentations, the intimidating door between me and the secret vinous society of winemaking had been cracked open. The harvest gig wasn't immediately lucrative by any means—driving forty-five minutes each way to the winery and being paid by check at a going rate of eight dollars an hour—but it far surpassed what I'd absorb from any college course on the subject.

Fast forward a couple years to winter of 2003 and I found myself back home on the central coast, separated, with two more wine harvests under my belt. I landed a full time job as a tasting room attendant for an Aussie wine lover named Gary Eberle at his namesake winery in Paso Robles. The former Penn State linebacker turned vintner stocked his cellar with as much

Australian wine as he did Bordeaux or Napa Valley, and was famous for being among the first to plant Syrah in California, as well as spearheading Paso Robles as a wine region to be reckoned with. I was slowly but surely picking up the pieces of my life then. At our staff Christmas party, Gary's treat was to send each employee down the spiral stairs to the cave beneath his house to pick out a wine to crack, with a few off-limits regulations. The first year I chose a 1994 Elderton Command Shiraz from Barossa Valley. It was the wine of the night, blowing doors off a Dunn Howell Mountain Cabernet and all others in its path. I found a shop in Atascadero that sold Command shortly after and bought the 1998 vintage for $60: the most I'd ever paid for a bottle of wine. The following year I grabbed the 1990 Henschke Mt. Edelstone Eden Valley Shiraz which was minty, full-bodied and even more sensational. The Father Christmas looking British tasting room manager at the party was beaming about the Australian selections. I read more and more into Australia's current wine scene and the country's rich history of ancient plantings of mostly Rhone grape varieties in the 1800's by colonists seeking to produce high alcohol and sweeter Port-style wines to export back to England at a fraction of the Portuguese price. Apparently, some of the oldest, gnarled, living vineyards in the world were in Australia. From what I gathered, dry, European-styled table wines from the largest producing state of South Australia didn't emerge into fashion until the 1980's. One critic kept referring to the current ripe, high alcohol style of Australia dry wines as "sunshine in a glass," with many of them suffering from too strong of an oak flavor from the use of brand new American oak barrels in the aging process. Wine critic Robert Parker was a champion of the new wave of Australia wines, and in his book entitled *World's Greatest Wine Estates* had an entire section devoted to wineries such as Penfolds, Burge Family, Torbreck, Jasper Hill and Noon, among others. These wineries were focused on dry, powerful wines made from grapes like Grenache, Shiraz, and Mataro, often blended together, with a decent amount of Cabernet Sauvignon in the mix and a few experimental varietals. With less financial burden in my newly single living situation, I was picking up Chateau Reynella Grenache on payday, splurging on a couple Hewitsons here and there, and as much of the Penfolds range as I could too.

In May 2004, I attended the Hospice Du Rhone festival in Paso Robles, where I sat in on the seminar of Clare Valley icons Kilikanoon and Pikes, tasted

Torbreck, Rolf Binder, D'Arenberg and some nicely aged Eileen Hardy's Shiraz, Leasingham's Classic Clare, and many others. I recall being floored by how the aged Australian wines dominated the older vintages tasting by looking, smelling and tasting fresh in the company of many brick colored and balsamic-like California wines. I romanticized the older Australian wines' longevity to some wonderful combination of old vines blossoming in a perfect grape growing climate. I learned the basics of making wine in California, but now I wanted to see for myself how to make wine with a ten-year life span in such historic wine land. That night of the Hospice du Rhone tasting, I dreamt of old vines, friendly blokes, emerald surf, girls who dug my American accent, kangaroos that could provide roadside directions, and getting as far away from my American reality as possible.

CHAPTER 2

The grape-flawed fiasco of 2008 up on the Sonoma Coast at Hirsch Vineyards deflated my winemaking gusto. Due to a battleground of June lightning storms that set fire to over 100 different locations in Mendocino County, a cough-inducing haze settled over the coastal ranges south of Anderson Valley, leaving serious compounds known as methylglyocol and guaiacol on the skins of developing 2008 vintage wine grapes. It was a major learning curve in many people's paths toward making fine wine. Any research into the matter and what could be done to remove smoke taint from wines before or after fermentation stemmed from Australia, and the remedies were meager at best. I remember the winemaker I worked under for my second harvest stint here hopelessly sitting in front of the computer as the problem became evident at Hirsch Vineyards, running a hand through his spiky, graying hair in agitation. The year before we had collectively produced some of the property's finest wines to date, and now this? Some wineries ended up using reverse osmosis on the wines after fermentation in attempt to blow off some of the smokiness. Others engaged in futile washing of the grapes prior to crushing them. But most just made a hell of a lot of rosé and bulk wine from a few of the most prized Pinot Noir sites in the Anderson Valley and Sonoma Coast.

At Hirsch, the winemaker Mick, nearby rancher Barbara and I made wine in the same high quality fashion as we did the year before, blindly hoping for the best, and, as the mustached, legendary vineyard owner David Hirsch put it, "keeping our noses in the tanks to see what's happening." It was strange to taste the flavors of chipotle salsa on the Pinot Noir grapes themselves as they came out of the crusher. Mick and I looked at each other, tasting these strange Southwestern flavors and exchanging a trouble-inparadise expression about the whole thing. As the fermentations started up in their various steel open top tanks, the smoky, old wetsuit aromas of the developing wines intensified, and the juice went from sweet to aggressively bitter in the mouth. This was one of the most expensive, famous vineyard sources for Pinot Noir in America and it was all going to hell. David's back went out soon after, and we saw the nasty side of him, as his entire year of efforts spiraled out of control. Having the most epic vinyl collection I'd ever seen and being a waltzing encyclopedia of old world wines, rock and jazz, David started snapping for us to turn down our modest CD player in the mornings. The press was acting up too and not squeezing the fermented skins to his desired gallonage, and he accused us of some conspiracy about it. Mick assured me that this version of David Hirsch had been there all along, but that I was too new and charmed to see it previously. The delectable year-round traveling sales position David had offered me at the end of harvest 2007 was never even brought up, and I was laid off in early November, with no real desire to taste anything we broke our spines over. At my parting meeting, David gave me my last check and said, "There you go Darren, and I gave you a tip too." It amounted to $300 after taxes.

I moved back into my friend Adam's house in San Luis Obispo, very much done with winemaking for possibly the long haul, and experimented with psychedelic music, psychedelics themselves, and a wild nine-month lust affair with Grace, the only nymphomaniac I've ever known. My quest to make great wine took a major back row seat to lust and gluttony. My nine months with her was a borderline scientific study into haunted human sexuality. Every other weekend I'd drive up to San Francisco, and two weeks later she'd come down. I couldn't walk properly and twice visited a chiropractor for a sex-related back injury. It was total, blurry insanity, which involved performing in a band called Asthmatic Giant and prep cooking at my mom's pizzeria just to finance this rendezvous. I stacked some night shifts at my dad's restaurant in Los Osos to compensate for all the driving and whatnot, which kept me afloat.

My dad, a former lover man in his own right, found the long distance thing amusing, since I hadn't ever introduced Grace to him, or to anyone in my family besides my mother once. I showed up for a shift unknowingly with bloody love bites all over my neck, and he told me to "button up."

Grace was an amazing cook, and I mentioned that when my dad asked about her best qualities that night at closing.

"You know son, that's far more important than looks when you get older. It's enough of a reason to stay with someone, that's for sure. But I've always told you, you could marry rich. Save yourself a lot of stress." He had a point.

In fall of 2009, an Australian wine lover on wine critic Robert Parker's message board named Jeremy Holmes, answered my post asking where to work in Australia during harvest where you can make some money, but more importantly make great wines. He suggested Yalumba, Rockford, and Two Hands. I applied for a 2010 harvest position with Two Hands Wines, a winery with Shiraz offerings that scored at the top of their game and was constantly featured all over the wine press. I got a great response and received a contract to look over a couple weeks later. The job would begin in early February 2010 and conclude in April or May, pay $1100 a week and include a staff meal every night. It also stated that the "vintage casuals" shouldn't work more than 12 hours a shift while receiving one day off a week. This looked beyond good to me, especially in comparison to what I endured at Hirsch, so I sent it back and got the confirmation from their winemaker Matt Wenk. It was all happening, much to the worry of Grace who confessed over a parting breakfast around that time that she had real feelings for me. Maybe I was finally exhausted from the arrangement. At the close of a two night stay, I limped out of her apartment like a 90-year-old man with bite marks all over my neck and arms. I needed freezer ice packs to sit on during the four-hour jaunts back home. Maybe I was living out some frantic high school era that I missed out on. I enjoyed her a lot, yet I wasn't willing to offer her anything more.

I hadn't entirely given up on winemaking that season. I made some small batch, overripe Sauvignon Blanc and Zinfandel from Saucelito Canyon Vineyard, a cold climate Syrah from Avila Beach, and an amusing single vine production of Roussanne from the Tablas Creek clone I planted in my mom's backyard. I made the wines sentimentally Hirsch style, with only the yeast nutrient of Fermaid K for fermentation. I learned it *is* possible to make a single bottle of wine off one vine, and in many ways, that was the point of everything in life.

Knowing Australia was on my horizon, Grace was trying to hold on, enticing me with a rendezvous in Laos when my May layoff came around. With my flight booked and a run-in with a blonde train wreck of a beach girl with the nickname of Spider Pig after a horrible gig in Avila Beach, I weaseled out of the relationship. By text. I justified it all by a cold quote I came up with: "relationships that begin electronically can end that way too." I ultimately called Grace and she kept saying I deceived her and never told her how I felt, and that there were CDs she needed mailed to her right away. Turns out that was all I had of hers in my possession after all that time. A series of emails afterward had her venting for the most part, saying my ex-wife had ruined me forever, and that I'll likely be old and alone acting like this to people. Maybe I would. But in a way, I was already in a jet airliner, en route to the lucky country.

CHAPTER 3

Hello Australia. How ya goin'? The tattooed, heavy metal-looking customs agent hassled me as much as a government man could in Sydney's International Airport. After getting through the first customs checkpoint, he pulled me aside to ask me about my plans for this four month "holiday" I mentioned I was on. Since my work visa wasn't yet approved for Two Hands Winery, I was told by winemaker Matt Wenk to buy a basic holiday visa and we'd sort out the work visa from Adelaide. Thus, I was only there for a holiday to the powers that be. Perhaps I should've rehearsed my plan, since apparently bearded folk troubadours my age don't often go on four-month walkabouts down under. Having eaten four pot cookies in 14 hours on my Qantas journey from Los Angeles, I wasn't as polished for this interrogation as I should have been, and my eyes must've looked like a dying man's.

"Do you got enough money to last you?" he asked me with a sneer, his black hair slicked back.

"Yeah, I think so."

"Are you planning to work? I see your occupation is listed as a winemaker."

"Not sure."

"Where will you be staying?"

"Tonight I've got a room in Glenelg."

"What are you planning on doing for four months?"

"Visit the wine regions, surf, check it all out."

"For four months."

"Yeah."

"Have you been to Australia before?"

"No. But I hear the people are cool."

"Do you know anyone in Australia?"

"No."

He reluctantly let me go, and the pilot on vacation from American Airlines that was seated next to me on the flight heard the exchange and scoffed at it as we proceeded across the Sydney airport to baggage claim. We got our bags down the way and I made it to the second customs checkpoint, where two girls checked my passport and ticket and told me to take my bags to an empty inspection counter across the room, much like a grocery store checkout. Moments later, that same customs agent strolled in. I was concerned now, and awfully glad I hadn't saved a cookie for when I got to the beach. Unless they tested my bowels for THC, I should've been free and clear for entry into Australia. He approached me with distrusting eyes and made a half-hearted fake attempt at acting like I'd never seen him before. The air thickened like old vine Grenache.

"I'm gonna have a look through your bags."

I hefted up my massive duffel bag and undid the lock, setting my backpack beside it. I noticed fellow passengers from my flight going right on through toward their connecting flight gates. Again, he started up with the same questions, as if this were our first encounter. I was vague about my plans, trying not to say much, which under the blurry circumstances was hard as hell.

"So your card says you're a winemaker. Are you coming here to work?"

"Not sure."

"What kind of visa did you get?"

"Oh a twenty dollar ETA one."

"And you have enough money to be here?"

"Yeah. Been planning this for awhile."

"How much do you have?"

"Oh seven thousand, in my account."

"Australia's expensive man. Seven grand?"

"I'm good at budgeting. I don't spend much."

"Let's have a look at your wallet."

I set it out there.

"How much money are you carrying?" He awkwardly reached over and opened up my wallet.

"Oh, a couple hundred dollars."

He started pulling out all of my belongings and I started to worry about whether he had record of my pending work visa. Maybe it was in their system? He pulled out the bubble wrapped bottles of Pinot Noir and looked at me. "What are these?"

"Oh wines from California. I hear you can't find any good California wine here."

"Are you bringing them for someone?"

"No I'll probably drink one tonight to celebrate being here."

He sneered. "Really?"

"Yeah."

He pulled out my bag of coffee beans, then my brown baritone ukulele. He held it up suspiciously.

"Are you a musician?" His eyes glared at mine as if the little hundred-dollar thing in his palms was a semi-automatic rifle.

"Yeah I play a little."

"What's this?"

"It's a harmonica and a holder for it."

"Really. Planning on playing some gigs here, for money, in Australia?"

"Oh I'm not that good. Maybe just show up at some open mics. Meet some musicians to play with."

He pulled my brand new cellar boots out next and looked at me hard. I nearly started whistling at that one. I was really getting the drift that I was going to get rolled here. It was unraveling before my very own bloodshot eyes.

"So you're telling me you are not here to work at a winery."

"Yeah. I mean, who knows, if I see signs for grape picking or whatever, like I've seen in France, maybe I will."

"You do know that if you don't have a work visa you will be deported for working."

"Yeah."

Then he pulled out my diary and set it next to his monitor and started flipping through the pages. The same diary from 2008 about my Hirsch Vineyard days and all out sluttiness. There were half-finished dark song lyrics in there, stuff about smoking and eating weed, self nurturing, sleeping with girls, etc... He started reading it quietly with his finger roving the page as I stood there. I watched him flipping pages, going to the end of it to check for most recent entries. I nearly wrote an entry on the flight over about coming to Australia to work for Two Hands in the Barossa, but I didn't. If there was ever any motivation for being lazy and not writing, this was it. I easily would've written my way into deportation.

"What is this?" he looked at me proudly.

"That's my diary."

He nodded and returned to reading.

"That's really personal," I pointed out.

"I know it's personal, but this is part of my job and the security of this country."

"Okay, but there's a lot of sex stuff in there, so don't get offended."

He nearly smiled then, but resisted it. Then he caught something in the front of the diary about working for Torbreck winery and having a hard time getting a work visa. He brought the diary over to me and pointed at my chicken scratch. He thought he had me.

"That's from two thousand and eight. I had a job but never made it over."

"Oh."

I pointed at the dated heading.

"So this year if you find a job will you be working?"

"Not sure."

"If you work, you will have to purchase a work visa first. Some places may pay you under the table, which is illegal, and you might get away with it. But if you're discovered doing that you will be deported and may never be granted a visa to enter Australia again."

I nodded.

"I'm going to have the wood of this instrument tested, and the coffee too."

I found it amusing to see my crappy baritone uke being taken so officially across the floor of the customs wing with its sheep sticker and LAMB LOVER written on it by this tough dude that clearly wanted the triumph of sending me home. The woman he showed it to came back over to the counter with him, and she tore into my bag of coffee with beans going everywhere. She muttered something in the affirmative and walked away.

"Okay, I am going to let you enter Australia." His facial expression was of a king who had just spared my life.

"Thank you."

"However, if you do work, you will be required to obtain a work visa first."

"Okay." He still had my diary out and my piece of paper with phone numbers and addresses on it.

"You can start putting your things away." He made a mock attempt to help me, but instead looked over that piece of paper. "What is Two Hands?"

"Oh a winery I really like."

"Are you going to be working there?"

"No."

I regretted saying that immediately. What if my work visa-in-progress was in their database? After reading a few more pages of my diary he gave me my things back.

"Is it rare to have someone my age vacation here for this long or something?"

"Yeah. I sometimes will check an account to ensure there's enough money for a length of stay." That just seemed illegal to me. He told me to enjoy myself and shook my hand.

"Yeah," I said. "I hear the people are cool."

* * *

"Bloody hell!" the white haired bus driver guy with bifocal glasses shouted upon sight of my huge duffel bag and me.

"Is this the bus to Glenelg?"

"Yeah mate. Where ya from?"

"California."

I paid the fare and sat right behind him, where a disabled or elderly passenger might sit, my childhood trauma of missing my stop haunting me at 33 years of age. There were some families on board, a few elderly passengers too. He was a friendly chatterbox and a welcome diversion to the first face of Australia that tried and failed to send me home. Once in the seaside touristy zone of Adelaide's most popular beach town, he let me off at the hostel and within earshot of every other passenger said "Enjoy our women, mate," as I descended onto the street.

I checked in at the bar, feeling rank from air travel, and got a key to my room, which was up the stairs with a street view. The town could have been Huntington Beach, with all the touristy eateries, beach goers on foot and on bikes, and families milling about in tank tops and flip flops. Amid the time difference it hardly seemed real. It was warm and humid out; it was still summertime in Australia after all. A strong wind was blowing onshore. I showered and got my room situated with intentions of sleeping, but couldn't. I wandered off to a bottle shop up the way and picked out a screw capped Petaluma Clare Valley Riesling from the cold case and brought it back to the hostel. I asked for a wineglass in the lobby and got denied: any booze drunk here had to be purchased here. The wines on hand looked iffy and surely oxidized, so I secretly ascended the stairs with my chilled bottle and proceeded to sip straight from the glass like a dirtbag, out on the balcony with my ukulele. After a glass or two's worth, I walked around the touristy town, found the beach, looked in at a few restaurants and bars, but the haze of jetlag had me in a dream, and the rest of the *rizza* put me to sleep in spite of the cigarette smoke and throbbing techno from the hostel bar below.

The next morning, an online Australian friend I'd made before leaving the states named Laura picked me up from the hostel to show me around McLaren Vale. I'd discovered her on the fan page of a cool Adelaide band called The Yearlings. She played banjo, booked shows occasionally, and worked at a winery in the Vale. Aside from her and the Two Hands Winery crew, I had no other contacts in this country. She was pale with long black hair and had a happy demeanor from the get go. Assuming I wasn't an ax-wielding American on the lam, she performed the role of ambassador for Australia rather well. She drove me down out of city limits to the bright and beautiful Fleurieu Peninsula in a trembling old van. She was an avid traveler herself and happy to help me see a bit of her hometown and wine valley before I started harvest. After getting past the virtual strangeness, we found ourselves to be on the same page, and we took my things to her stylish little beach house in Noarlunga. "Something died in the roof of my house I think," she prefaced as we parked out front, "so I apologize if it smells."

"Like what?"

"A possum maybe. Don't know." She went inside first, sprayed some air freshener, and flagged me in. I arranged my bags in the living room and we were out the door again, heading down to McLaren Vale to go tasting. We talked about music, her career in the cellar door field of the industry, and about the show she arranged for me to play at in Adelaide that coming

Sunday in support of The Yearlings. We entered the wine zone and it was strange to see bird netting on vines in February. Harvest was approaching while vineyards in California looked abandoned.

We visited her former place of employment first: Maxwell's Winery. As I tasted with the friendly cellar door attendant, Laura used the phone to get a hold of her wine writer friend that she really wanted me to meet. Some Asian tasters came in for the mulled cider Maxwell's specialized in, which the woman had to heat up on a little burner behind the counter to serve. I couldn't imagine having to do that. I didn't buy anything. I was still time warped and wondering if this was a dream or if I was really wine tasting in Australia.

Afterward we drove into the wooded, rural McLaren Flat area and she pulled off at a deli and urged me to consume a sandwich, or anything, before our next stop: the residential shack of Mr. Philip White, South Australia's notorious wine scribe. We entered Yangarra Winery's property around 3 PM and rattled up to a small dwelling with a covered patio where a long haired, cigarette-smoking man relaxed at a table awaiting our arrival. A skull earring dangled from his right lobe. He was stout in stature, eyes turquoise blue, and he greeted me earnestly, reminding me of an aged Russell Crowe. There was an opened bottle of Mitolo Sangiovese Rosé out on the table. Soon I'd learn that the man was a poet, philosopher, political speechwriter, wine blogger, and musical historian as well as a songwriter. The rosé, with its cherry aromatics and mostly dry, watermelon flavor profile, quenched our collective thirst as the afternoon wind started to blow the heat around. His mirrored Highway Patrolman style shades were propped up on his receding hairline and constantly fell down over his eyes as each full-bodied laugh erupted. His little house was full of instruments, dozens of wine samples set out on tables, vials of single malt scotch for review, and troves of books, magazines and manuscripts. It all painted the picture of a secular, life-loving, new world Hemingway. Or, with the alcohol on hand taken into equation, perhaps a more presentable Charles Bukowski. He'd met the Beats, knew the hippies, been through romantic hellfire, and interviewed every famous rock and roll musician who set foot down under in the 1970's for a Sydney newspaper. He soon was a stumbling vault of celebrity lore, both Hollywood and the winemaking type. Laura mentioned on the way over that he drinks from noon on with an ever-growing affinity for gin come nightfall. As the afternoon became evening, the charcuterie plate was swept clean and the delicious bottle of rosé and a few others were well drained, I felt half-initiated into the world of South Australian wine, complete with the unveiling of his intensive geology map of McLaren Vale, the idea of which he first percolated back in 1974. We stood over the dining room table with it spread out before us.

"It's quite confronting," he said. "McLaren Vale is the midpalate of South Australian wines. It's time for them to start making better wines." He mentioned neighbors who were watering to achieve monstrous eight to ten tons per acre grape loads, and praised the new six-million-dollar winery that Jess Jackson and Barbara Banke had just completed for Yangarra within eyeshot of Philip's front patio. The man was full of expletives, analogies, and hilarious clichés. In fact, he possessed the most profane mouth I'd ever heard. I had to stand back and laugh at it at times, looking to Laura who'd just raise her eyebrows in slight apology. This was what I was looking for. Thanks to this man and Laura, I'd just experienced one of those surreal afternoons in another country where you get high, meet a member of Parliament, see a grown man make out with a horse, and grow blind off Shiraz, Nebbiolo and Cabernets from labels you've never seen before.

At dusk, record producer and Mixmasters Studio owner Mick Wordley pulled up after Laura and Philip had phoned him and invited him over, and I got the baritone ukulele out of the van. Laura had raved to me about Mick, who was in his salt and peppered late 40's and was a talented performer, engineer, vintage guitar collector, and all around cool, friendly guy. His taste in music was apparently right in line with ours. The jamming started straight away. With Philip being a huge Grateful Dead and Bob Dylan fan, and Mick's knowledge of every Neil Young song ever released, the table of contents was wide open. Maybe we were to blame for the lag time of the alleged dinner Philip was making us, because every time we got into a song like "Brown Eyed Women" or "The Weight," he had to stop barbecuing to come over and join us in the chorus, then tell an anecdote about partying with people like Leonard Cohen when they toured Australia back in the day. "Leonard was a dirty, dirty man!" he shared. It was fascinating. We were drunk. Our stomachs were running on purple. Acid reflux was kicking in and I lost track of the time, date and place. Close to midnight, we moved the party inside for the pork belly spice course. I ate cautiously, pea by pea. I noticed Philip didn't eat his at all.

I laughed from the moment we sat down at the dinner table till I was drifting away at 3 AM to the sounds of he and Mick Wordley drinking fortified Shiraz and playing one of Philip's original songs. It was dedicated to an ex-lover about doing her a favor and dying first so he can "be in a casket built for two and waiting for you." Then they started strumming Dylan's "Peggy Day" and I passed out next to Laura on the floor of his office.

The next morning I came out of the bathroom to see Philip standing in the kitchen boiling water. "Morning," I said to him.

"Is that what you call this?" he mumbled. Mick had ducked out. He made coffee for us and the talk turned to literary subjects. I mentioned that writing was one of my main interests in life, and he pulled out old copies of City Lights Press and told a story about how he was in charge of hosting the beats when they first came to Australia on a book tour. "Allen Ginsberg kept trying to fuck me, the whole fucking time. And finally I said to him, 'Allen! Get fucked!'"

As we got up to leave, Philip looked me in the eye and said "You're too good of a guitar player for Two Hands, mate. Be careful up there." I wasn't sure what he meant by that, but I got the drift that he wasn't a big fan of the company I was here to work with.

* * *

Laura and I headed up to meet her mom Claire and her stepdad John in the seaside town of Port Willunga where they resided. They had a tropical, two-story oasis in a hilly neighborhood blocks from the beach. Claire was sweet from the start and thrilled to feed a traveling American. She was from Scotland and moved to Oz when Laura was two years old. After 27 years of marriage, she fished through her husband's briefcase and discovered a series of love letters to him from his mistress. He moved out and she held a saucy divorce party in this house, in which John walked over to with a six-pack of Guinness. Twelve years later they had a very sweet, unique relationship going.

John was a fit schoolteacher with bleached spiky hair from his daily swim routines in the ocean. We drank through cups of coffee on the top balcony overlooking an emerald coastline and the lumpy dry hills of McLaren Vale. There was a large reef offshore that ran parallel to the tideline, allowing a calm interior for sun worshipers and John's daily swims. It looked like Hawaii. Claire laid out a spread of epicurean delights: cheeses, olives, and spinach quiche. We first drank a Shottesbrooke Merlot, and then a "cleanskin" unlabeled Shiraz from Samuel's Gorge.

Her folks' house had a southeast Asia vibe to it, complete with bright, tribal artwork, plants everywhere, and groovy trinkets of the like. They were globetrotters themselves and fancied vacation over work more than most. When they spoke to me and asked me questions, it was in earnest and engaging, with no superficiality about it. Only three days in and the stereotype about the welcoming and kind nature of the Australian people was proving true.

Laura took me for a walk down to the cliff's edge at sunset, which lingers longer here than in California it seemed, where I opened up the Brewer-Clifton Pinot Noir I flew over. *It's just so different,* Laura kept saying as we were drinking it, overlooking a pier and jetty. The weather had cooled to golden perfection, and for an ocean front street in the summertime on a Saturday night, it was peacefully quiet, aside from the odd carload of what Laura referred to as "bogans." The setting was awfully romantic, yet I defied going in that direction. It was a test. Couldn't I just be friends with a cool individual and not have to ruin it by taking things further?

Back at the house, John put on "Music from Big Pink" by The Band on vinyl, Steve Earle's "Townes" record, Dennis Wilson's solo album, and Monsters of Folk. In the company of Claire and John, I realized how weird and unrelaxed my own restaurateur parents were, but I couldn't blame them for it. Blame America and its unobtainable dream. My parents never took time off.

I tuned up Laura's acoustic guitar in the garden area and played a nervous round of tunes for everybody. Claire kept asking for the harmonica I brought along. I played "Don't Think Twice it's all right," "Seems so long ago, Nancy" by Leonard Cohen, and "Black and Brown Blues" by the Silver Jews.

When I finished, Laura asked, "So are you ready for your show tomorrow?"

"Yeah I think so," I said, sweating and shaking.

She assured me that people at the Wheatsheaf Hotel are into the same music that we are, and that it should be great. Along the way, Laura's mom got hammered, and soon was incomprehensibly asking me questions and saying things none of us could understand, not even John.

"When do you start up?" John asked about my Two Hands job as I set the guitar back into its case.

"Monday at eight."

"How many days a week?"

"The contract says six days a week, twelve hours a day max."

"Daz, never work more than four days a week. That's my advice to ya. And even that's too much. Remember that."

CHAPTER 4

Malibu's Timmy Thompson picked me up as planned at The Wheatsheaf Hotel on Sunday. With blonde hair, photogenic looks, and a slight aloofness to his demeanor, he asked if it was okay to shoot some film while I performed on stage. I introduced him to Laura, and to Robyn and Chris from The Yearlings, with whom Laura and I caught a lift into Adelaide. Mick Wordley, who I met and jammed with at Philip White's shack, was there with his wife Robin too. I sat down with him for a bit and we talked about which wineries he liked in Barossa Valley and if he had any contacts up there, wine or music related. He wrote down the name of his mate who he suggested I look up in the Barossa. "He makes incredible wines, some of the best," he assured me, handing me over the small piece of paper with "Rick Burge, Burge Family Winemakers" written across it.

Timmy had bought a car for two grand in Melbourne and driven the Great Ocean Road over to Adelaide, sleeping in it and getting a speeding ticket along the way. He had just finished his film degree at the University of Santa Barbara, and over a beer I came to learn that we knew a lot of the same wine people in Santa Barbara County. I did a 30-minute acoustic set of mostly original music for about twenty or so people in the smoldering hot room, a result of the daily high temp and the patio heaters accidentally being on full blast. With the daylight dwindling and the roads up to Australia's most famous wine valley foreign to us, I decided that Timmy and I should leave halfway through The Yearlings' set. I found Laura at the bar talking to a girlfriend of hers with jet black bangs like Uma Thurman in *Pulp Fiction*, got briefly introduced, then gave Laura a long hug goodbye and a sincere thanks for everything. I said I'd be in touch, even though I didn't have a phone or any transportation.

Timmy and I drove out onto one of the main roads in his little red four door, and, judging by the direction of the sun, headed north through a very industrial, working man's part of the city.

"I'm going to need to get gas I think," Timmy said straight away. "I'm pretty much on e." Knowing how much the Barossa Valley Coach would've cost me, I happily pitched in thirty dollars and he seemed grateful. "Thirty? I'm going to get a meat pie with some of the cash now."

After filling up, he pulled back out onto the road and devoured his gas station delicacy. We started talking about the accommodation winemaker Matt had found for the two of us to live in during harvest. It was a room on a vineyard at a guy named Aaron's place, and we were going to be moving in that evening.

Timmy insisted that we try to call Matt for the address or more details at least, so I used his phone to call. Matt picked up and even his "hello" was hard to understand. I needed subtitles for his responses a minute in. Our email interactions had been full of humor, but on the line I wasn't sure I really deciphered much of anything. Timmy was concerned about directions to the Barossa first and foremost. Matt said Timmy had already called earlier for directions and gotten in touch with Aaron before the show. Amid the Aussie speak I got the confirmation that we were set to start work at 8:30 the next morning, and to look out for a forthcoming cross street. "Yeah easy," Matt said a couple times.

As we hit the countryside and got our first glimpse of green Barossa vines in the golden light of the late afternoon, Timmy had me film from the passenger seat. My handheld technique surely created footage to puke to, but maybe he'd get some use out of it for a film he was planning on making about working the harvest. We drove through a few historic looking small towns, with the dry, yellow patches of countryside holding the promise of the brown snakes, redback spiders and other deadly Australian critters I'd researched online.

We drove beneath a massive banner with the Jacob's Creek winery logo on it, as if they sponsored the entire township of a place called Tanunda. Timmy had me call Aaron, who was much easier to understand than Matt. He said he would meet us in a town called Angaston at the pub called the Brauhouse. "We gonna do a bit of drinking?" I asked.

"Nah. I had a big night last night, mate, so yea, we'll meet there, have a beer, then I can take ya out to the house."

Turns out the Brauhouse was attached to a mini casino and a wine shop. We stepped into the L-shaped bar area and two burly, older guys and the bartender just stared at us. We didn't know what Aaron looked like, and the same went for him, though the two Californians must have looked pretty obvious. We walked through the bar area, past the pool tables, then resorted to browsing the unrefrigerated wine selection in the shop upstairs, the bottles hot to the touch. After buying a Clare Valley Riesling out of the refrigerator, we searched the pub again and, as we sheepishly ordered a round, a sleeveless, big-armed guy came up to us and introduced himself. Aaron was slightly younger than me, had blonde hair and looked a bit like a surfer, even though my research put the Barossa about two hours away from any wave worthy coastline. Moments later, Aaron's mother-in-law joined us outside with a drink to gauge us before moving in to what was technically her house, and she smoked through numerous cigarettes with her son-in-law and gave us the rundown of her three available daughters and pretty much matched Timmy up with her 21-year-old sight unseen. "She's gonna like this one," she said with a nod to Timmy. She wasn't quite sold on me yet, squinting at me through an exhale of smoke, and more power to her.

We finished our beers and followed them back out to their property in the Eden Valley, passing historic Yalumba winery along the way. It was higher elevation in this part of the territory, with oak-like trees and vineyards stretching across the hillsides. Once we arrived at our new address, we slowly stepped out to see what we were in for. There was a large single story house to the left, a barbecue, refrigerator, and sink outside and some haggard patio furniture on the concrete. Off the hill was a stellar view across a canyon with no houses in the distance. Aaron introduced us to his wife Steff who was drinking a beer outside, and we were assigned a detached, freshly painted white fume box across from the main house that was just like my shack at Hirsch Vineyards, but with bunk beds and without a kitchenette or a fridge.

"So it's a grand a month," Aaron announced as the three of us stood there. Timmy gave me a worried look, and at 33 years of age I had to say that dwelling in bunk beds would be ridiculous no matter what the price.

To their defense, Aaron's wife Steff cooked us up some welcoming steak sandwiches and Aaron cracked one of the best Cabernets I'd had in a year's time: Eden Springs 2006 High Eden. Dark, non-green with cocoa notes, resolved chocolaty tannins, and seamless. Timmy wasn't so convinced, but I proceeded to smash two thirds of the bottle. Then he opened a more expensive, herbal 2007 Barossa appellation Cabernet as we talked about drugs and his and Steff's recent drug-rattled honeymoon through Europe. He said he had a friend that could find me weed, but was more interested in the surprising array of pills Timmy brought over.

Aaron worked for a large, factory wine operation called Rocland Winery on the edge of nearby Nuriootpa, and he told us Two Hands rented a large section of the place for barrel storage and case goods storage. The place sounded massive, with holding tanks the size of hotels, producing hundreds of different labels of wine. And Steff was apparently one of the best machine harvest operators in the valley, contracting with multiple wineries and vineyards to get grapes off the vine, mostly at night. They were a solid combination and had plans to launch their own family label of higher end wines.

Before we turned in, Timmy tried to negotiate a cheaper rent from Aaron. We were 20 minutes away from work, out in the sticks, and if Timmy didn't have a car to commute to work in, we'd both be screwed by the locale.

"Yeah I'll talk to Steff about it," Aaron said. "Should be all good. Maybe even throw the first week in free."

We didn't realize it was just the local purple booze talking.

I got situated in the bottom bunk with headphones on and started scribbling in my journal. The night before starting a winery harvest gig could be as nerve wracking as it was exciting. All the winery knew about us came from resumes and references. Machinery would be different. Winemaking techniques too. There was always a bit of fear and anxiety for me, wondering if I had what it takes to get through it all. Timmy climbed up top with his laptop and after a minute said, "Hey, did you get online? I can't get online."

CHAPTER 5

I beat Timmy to the shower in the morning, waking up to a fire red sunrise over the Eden Valley. But I wasn't alone. While toweling off I noticed a massive tarantula eye level on the shower door top. It'd been there the whole time as I washed up. I put on jeans and a t-shirt and warned Timmy on his way in. He got his camera out and filmed me smashing it to pieces. "Sorry man, I have a kill-on-sight policy when it comes to spiders and insects in my living space," I clarified while bludgeoning the thing with my Doc Marten.

We drove into Angaston and stopped off at the namesake bakery. I ran across the street and grabbed a coffee from Blond Coffee. Fed and caffeinated, we arrived at the Two Hands Marananga facility at 8:30 and saw Matt Wenk dressed in a dark blue Two Hands work shirt, shorts and boots, talking to a young tan fella in the lot. We passed some old head trained vines on the way in, many of them dead and gone. We stepped out into the Barossa heat and shook hands in the lot. The young guy with an iron shake was Calie from South Africa, who was a cellar casual like us. We went inside the cool temperature controlled office building. A lanky woman with short cropped graying hair named Amanda was inside the break room. She ran many operational parts of the winery, including HR and compliance. She seemed amused to meet us, smirking as we told her who we were and where we were from, and she soon advised us to go upstairs and begin our new employee paperwork at the conference table. We passed by an older, wild-eyed mutt named Holly, who looked at us wearily from the top of the stairwell. At the long table already filling out the forms was a freckled girl with sandy blonde hair named Chelsea from New Zealand. Matt sat down with us and we had a jovial chat while we filled out our forms. Amanda came up and urged us to check out any of the forthcoming cultural events in Adelaide while we could, like the Fringe Festival and WOMAD. She said previous cellar casuals have tended to stay in Barossa and just worked and drank, without seeing any of the city or the beach communities to the south. She had a very theatrical way about her as she talked and explained things, and immediately came across as an ally. Matt told me to hold off e-filing for an Australian tax id number, which could send out a red flag to immigration, as my work visa was still yet to be approved. I told him of my hassles coming in. Matt thanked me for letting him know, so he could inform one of the other cellar casuals named Michael who was older than me and still in California awaiting his work visa approval. Apparently he had to pay to change his ticket because of the hang up.

After the forms were completed, Matt introduced the General Manager named Phil who sat at the head of the table beside him. The red headed Englishman went over the documents and signed off on them. Then Matt passed out booklets full of winery protocol, from yeast selections, acid additions, oak preferences, to tasks such as pressing and barreling down, to the goals of vintage 2010. "Quality without Compromise" was printed on multiple pages of it.

"We're crushing some Chardonnay at Branson today, and some Fronti, so we can have a bit of a look at that," Matt said. His eyes darted around a bit throughout the morning, as if there was something mulling about under the surface. "It'll be a relatively easy day."

Timmy and I attempted to follow Matt, Chelsea and Calie in their Two Hands company vehicle and got lost on a dirt road. We pulled over by a vineyard as Timmy tried to call Matt. It was baking outside, little white and grey puffy clouds with perfectly flat bottoms suffering in the blue sky. Matt came back for us, and we drove over to the unmarked Branson winery facility. I was more apprehensive than excited by this point. This property used to be some kind of vineyard and winery of its own, but now the cellar door at the entrance looked like a bombed out homeless encampment. Windows were smashed out, walls were cracked, and weeds were growing up to the roofline. There was a broken and faded sign that read "Branson Coach House Winery." The production area at the rear of the property was more maintained, with large tanks lined up outside on a concrete foundation. We parked and walked up to problems. Two guys in fluorescent orange jerseys gave Matt the update. The white wine press was loaded with grapes and wasn't working. I looked up at the strangest production zone I've ever seen. In a triangular building three stories high hung eight massive open top steel tanks over the bird-shit stained concrete slab below. They were cylindrical cones in shape, held in place by metal railings, and would simply be illegal in any country that had earthquakes. The area stunk like dead animals. We looked up to see dozens of pigeons flapping around above those tanks, with nests wedged into the roof's interior.

We were introduced to Ben Perkins, who appeared to have some sort of managerial role. He greeted us awkwardly and without any break for getting-to-know you chat. He said we could start by washing tanks. So this is what "having a look at" meant. The introductory tour was over. It was time to get to work. Another casual named Kim from Napa Valley had already been working here for a week, so she showed us the chemical protocol in regards to cleaning hoses, tanks, pumps, etc. She was sharp and had things figured out fast it seemed. I started right in on one of the outside steel tanks, and the process slowly came back to me, with the usual moments of spacing out. I ended up working my way down a row of four tanks, cleaning most of them as the day moved along. At one point, Ben came around to check on me.

"I heard you worked at Hirsch," he said.

"Yeah, in 2007 and 2008. Have you worked in California?" I asked.

"For Thomas Rivers Brown in Napa. Outpost and Rivers-Marie, and Michael's wine too."

"Michael Twelftree? From Two Hands?"

"Yeah he does Two Worlds Cab there."

"Did you like it? Working there?"

Timmy interrupted to ask Ben about the cleaning protocol and a green lemon scented paste called JIF that we were cleaning tanks and hoses with. It seemed like everyday dish soap instead of a winery grade cleaning agent more commonly used back in the states. "Are we really using this?" Timmy asked him, holding up the small plastic JIF container in his hand. Ben walked away with him to the corrugated paneled indoor tank room to give him a demonstration.

Just before sunset, Matt arranged for five large pizzas for the crew, and we laid them out at Branson on the desk and had a communal feast among the flies. He also procured a bottle of Russian vodka for his vintage ritual of Moscato Martinis: freshly pressed tropical White Frontignac juice mixed with Vodka over ice.

After work, Timmy and I went grocery shopping. He repeatedly mentioned his financial state of distress after buying the red Magna, and was hinting at going in on groceries, which I opted not to do. We charged into the Foodland supermarket in Tanunda and grabbed baskets. I beelined for the produce section and he went ahead of me, only to double back and see what I was up to. We reconvened at the checkout line and he only had cereal and milk in his basket.

When we got back to the property and put our food away in the outside fridge, Timmy double-checked the rent situation with Aaron. Not good. Steff was sticking with the original price after all, but the first week would be a slightly reduced $50 each. Timmy said he couldn't do it, and now there was tension brewing. I was complacent, having picked up a half ounce of hydroponic cannabis for 100 bucks. Timmy wouldn't quit though. It was like we were at a Mexican street fair the way he insistently pushed Aaron on the issue over the course of the evening, no matter what else we started talking about. In our bunk beds that night, Timmy formulated a plan to look for something else ASAP. I was stoned and on the bottom bunk with nostrils burning from the drying paint. Being confined to his vehicle, I'd go wherever was needed, but the local anesthetic certainly helped in the flexibility department.

CHAPTER 6

After another morning of attempting to sanitize the Branson facility, the cellar casuals started in on a barrel tasting around 11 AM with Matt in Marananga. He used a small hose to siphon us glasses of the 2009 vintage that was resting in the large barrels that were referred to as Hogsheads, which were 75 liters bigger than a standard barrel. Almost all of the barrels were made of French oak, as opposed to the old Australian norm of using sweeter American oak. We were spitting our tastes into a silver pail on the cellar floor at the center of our circle, and just as we were comparing old vine and young vine Shiraz from the same vineyard up in the Clare Valley, a big man in a Two Hands cap, blue polo shirt, shorts and leather loafers stepped in with a glass unannounced.

"What are we on here Matt?" he asked, holding out an empty glass.

"Young vine Bunny," Matt said, pouring him a sample.

"Bunny Peglidis!" the man shouted. We tasted through ten more hogsheads of Shiraz, spitting into the pail, palates annihilated by the blackness of each wine, before the man took the siphon hose from Matt and asked, "Are you ready for the best thing you've ever put in your mouth?" We snickered as he went off and pulled a sample of some 2008 Cabernet Sauvignon that was black as night. He talked at length about the kinds of wines he liked to make and drink, and kept putting Matt on the spot for answers, all the while never introducing himself. I knew who he was though: owner Michael Twelftree. I'd read his posts over the years on Robertparker.com, and even emailed him on there to inquire about working at Two Hands in 2008. In the winery's promotional photos, he looked like a guy who used to play rugby: big and as bold as the packaging that held these wines together.

A long table was set up in the cellar behind us with polished wine glasses and platters of sausage and ribs soon placed on it. Finishing the tasting with the 2008 Ares Shiraz that was about to be bottled, Michael said it was time for lunch. There were bottles on the table bearing labels I'd never seen before. He opened them and poured a glass of Riesling for himself, sitting down at the table. Timmy was the first to go over and introduce himself and praise the Two Hands wines. "Ah, are you the surfer?" Michael asked Timmy.

"Me? No. That'd be Darren." I looked over and the man was smiling at me.

"I saw photos," Michael said. "Impressive. Who's the musician?"

"That's me too," I said. My coworkers were having a look at me.

"Ahh I see." We each lined up to shake his hand then and introduce ourselves. Ben sat next to Michael as we had a massive feast. Current releases of Two Hands wines were on the table, but at Michael's end there were some other famous wines by Giaconda, Rockford, and Moss Wood that never got passed down. I was just assured to know that this was actually one of those mythical, breezy days during a wine harvest gig where barrel tasting and a long lunch were the only items on the agenda. I'd heard of them all the time but had never worked anywhere that got around to having one.

* * *

Aaron and Steff's place got struck by lightning in the tropical storm that afternoon. Timmy and I were getting shocked on everything we touched—the shower, opening the fridge, doing laundry, and turning on a sink—before we realized that rubber sandals were the solution. Aaron described the scene as "full on off the richter" on the phone to the local electrician, who showed up ten minutes later for the service call with a 12 pack of beer. The inch-long black and red ants were out for our flesh since it had rained. I fried up potatoes and a lamb steak to go with the bottle of Eden Springs Cabernet Aaron sold me for 20 bucks, which was a hustle on his part but better than me paying retail price. Steff said we could eat inside their place to dodge the random rainfall. The wine had the nose of a Beaulieu Vineyard Napa Valley Cab I had when I was first getting into wine, and was plush, minty, low acid, and full of coffee and mocha richness. A seamless wine with integrated tannins. I dodged Timmy's request for more of it, since he hadn't picked up any wine or beer yet, but seemed to be drinking everybody else's. He was sniffing around for some of my lamb dinner too after having merely a bowl of cereal. I drank most of the bottle at Aaron and Steff's dinner table by myself while I ate. Steff left shortly afterward for a machine harvest night pick while Aaron and the electrician were still outside drinking and working on the power situation.

There was a skinny, quiet New Zealander named Greg who was working for Aaron at the Rocland Winery and living in the main house with Aaron and Steff. Greg had furry brows and worried eyes, and would pop out of his room to exchange pleasantries, then retreat. The first night here, he talked about how he was planning on taking his girlfriend to Asia for a holiday when he finished up the vintage. He snuck out to say "hi" while I was alone and washing my dishes. He asked how I was liking working for Two Hands. I told him it was good so far and mentioned the tasting and luncheon of the day. He took that in with a serious nod and then excused himself for the night.

Aaron's mate turned up around 8 PM with a cleanskin 2005 Barossa Shiraz from his dad's vineyard that was powerful but could've used a chill down in the heat. These local wines were so big that if the serving temperature wasn't right, all you could smell was alcohol. Before Aaron tried it, he fetched a bottle of the upcoming Goodchild Shiraz he'd made to compare. I was happy to see this side of the wine culture here. It was like an unwritten law that if you show me yours I show you mine, but it was done with good intentions. Timmy and I were able to join in and we sat outside with Aaron and his buddy, tasting the two wines side by side. I brought up the ants again, how massive and angry they seemed, and Aaron told us a story of how a friend of his passed out drunk in his chair on the patio and woke up covered with hundreds of them, mostly in crevices, with bites, welts and everything.

"Good to know," I said, keeping my feet off the floor.

CHAPTER 7

On Thursday we got the heads up from Ben on a motel in Tanunda that had cheap weekly rates. The ad was in the local paper. I called the motel on my morning break at Branson and talked to a guy named Chris, who said his place was right on Barossa Valley Highway and that single units were going for $190 a week. "How much for a double?" I asked.

"Uh, mate I could do a double for, I dunno, two hundred?"

"Two hundred a week total?" I said out loud, much to Timmy's standby excitement.

"But the thing is there's a weekend that we're fully booked, for the concert, so you'd have to move out for that weekend, but ya'd be back in by that Sunday night. Easy."

"We'll come by and have a look today," I said.

We began our machinery training with the crushing and pressing of ten tons of White Frontigniac for the "Brilliant Disguise" Moscato. The faulty bladder press was finally loaded with the entire lot around quitting time for the casuals. A chubby Germanic Aussie named Heintje arrived in the early afternoon on a motorcycle to handle the nightshift that the late pressing called for. Heintje was the other full-time cellar hand, along with Nathan, who Kim and Calie were renting rooms from in Tanunda. Heintje had been working solo at Rocland all week, topping and sulfuring hogsheads full of 2009 vintage wines that were soon to be bottled, so this was our first encounter with him. He looked like a punk rocker with the sides of his head shaved, gold hoop earrings, and a cherub face that disarmed him. He was shy and mumbled a lot like Matt did, but I noticed a trend where he'd attempt a quick joke or some humor and follow it right up with a nervous snort.

Ben came along with Timmy and I to have a look at the potential new accommodation. We found the well marked entrance and pulled into the gravel world of the Barossa Junction Motel. Once inside the office we met Chris the manager, who was friendly, around my age, with a slight mullet and wearing a green polo shirt, jeans and white running shoes. There was a little stuffy bar and a pool table, though it wasn't open for business, and probably hadn't been for awhile. To the left of the check-in counter was a large commercial kitchen space that was also out of commission. "Let's go suss the double out," Chris said and we stepped outside the office.

To our surprise, the rooms were a series of old blue or green train cars sitting on rails and converted into the funkiest motel rooms I've ever seen. There were over 30 of them in a u-shaped track formation, with a tennis court, funky miniature golf course, and an indoor pool and spa. After a few nights in the country with bunk beds, fumes, ants of Satan, tarantulas, and complimentary shock treatment, the comforts of motel living with a TV, maid service, in-room refrigerator, internet and fresh towels seemed like a dream come true. Timmy and I looked at each other and confirmed that we'd take it. We could move in the following afternoon. Aaron and Steff were not going to dig the news that night.

We drove back excitedly to Eden Valley, and I mentioned to Timmy that we might want to announce our move out at the end of the evening, if not the next day as we actually moved out. We hadn't paid anything yet. Timmy seemed to be in agreement of that. We pulled up to the property and saw Aaron outside drinking a beer. I grabbed my dirty clothes and walked over to start a load of laundry. Aaron started complaining about how much fruit they already got in at Rocland, and how the day was hectic with both equipment and human failures. He offered us beers and Timmy accepted one. I poured myself a glass of Riesling out of the fridge. As Timmy wrapped his fingers around the beer bottle, he smiled at Aaron and happily spilled the beans. "We found a place in town! We're moving out tomorrow."

Aaron was shocked. I cringed. So much for the agreement. "Goddamnit, Timmy" I thought. Aaron looked at me and I couldn't even hold eye contact with him. It was a betrayal. We'd become friends in these few nights together, drinking and smoking and laughing. "It's just so close to work man," I said.

"How much?" Aaron asked.

"A hundred each," Timmy said.

"Okay, well… Cool. Okay."

Steff came out soon after, dressed for work.

"Whoa you're going to work now?" I asked.

"Yeah. It's full on. We've been harvesting since six last night. We're gonna go till at least six tomorrow." She and Aaron exchanged a serious look, and then she asked him for a lift.

When they were gone, Timmy and I started making our respective meals in their kitchen. Greg appeared with worried eyes.

"Hey Greg, how was your day?" I asked.

"Oh man. Did they say anything?" he asked us.

"What do you mean?" Timmy said.

"Aaron and Steff."

"Nah man. What happened?"

"I quit today."

"You quit?" I asked, making guacamole.

"It wasn't what I expected. I was going crazy."

I was in his shoes once before, at the start of the 2007 harvest at Hirsch Vineyard, and I almost quit before things really started up. My main issue there was a personality conflict, though there was a great deal of frustration that came with working in a new place with foreign equipment, dealing with the monotony of sanitizing endless tanks and hoses, and the pressure of how busy and work bound you were about to become when the grapes arrived. One of the lowest moves you can make in the wine industry is signing on to work a wine harvest and then quitting, especially at the start. Greg could have been employed by a coal mine as much as a winery, since his master plan was simply stacking hours for the money to spend on a romantic vacation at the end of it all. You had to have passion for this, even to do it on a factory-sized winemaking level, just to get through it.

"I think they're pissed at me," he added. "Steff's mom went off on me this afternoon. Told me she couldn't believe that I'd do this to them, especially when Aaron's grandfather is dying. Went off full on."

"His grandfather's dying?" I asked.

"Yeah I guess." He had his arms wrapped around himself, telling us the news.

"Are you going to look for something at a smaller winery?" Timmy asked him.

"I don't know."

He was a nervous wreck. Pacing. Crazy eyes. What a day for announcements in this household. I'm surprised Aaron didn't snap on us for breaking our news. "Do you want a glass of wine?" I asked him.

"Nah. I-I don't know what I'm gonna do."

"We're moving out tomorrow," Timmy added.

Greg went back into his room and closed the door. Timmy and I ate and cleaned up. An hour later Greg fled with his things, waiting on the side of the road in the dark with all his gear packed up, waiting for some fellow Kiwis to pick him up in a state of emergency. When I came back in to wash my wine glass, I saw his note on the table written out to Steff and Aaron. He was gone.

CHAPTER 8

On Friday morning all of the cellar casuals went on a field trip to some of the Barossa Valley vineyards with Matt. He and Michael wanted us to really see where the fruit was going to be coming from, which were mainly smaller, really high quality vineyards. I assumed there'd be some massive factory-sized farms that some of the Shiraz was going to be harvested from, but we looked at Tammy's Vineyard, which was close to Marananga and had rows planted tightly together to minimize vigor and produce concentrated clusters, then the sloping face of Shobbrook Vineyard where the John Lennon doppelganger Tom Shobbrook found us and introduced himself after we'd walked around. He wore a t-shirt, beige shorts and Birkenstock sandals, with circular wire-rimmed glasses on and brown hair tied back into a ponytail. The vineyard, owned by his father, was utilizing biodynamic farming methods, which in short is organic gardening and witchcraft combined. The grapes were tart to the taste, even though the skins were mostly purple. Michael said we were weeks away from harvesting any Barossa Valley Shiraz, and that McLaren Vale vineyards further south tend to ripen first. We looked at some old Grenache vineyards afterward that were frazzled by the springtime frost and not holding many clusters because the developing buds had been fried. Those vines would have to be hand picked because of the variability. We were getting the drift that Barossa Valley wasn't all sunshine and easy grape growing year after year, and Michael brought up the weather events that have affected recent vintages. Seemed like the last easy year that produced outstanding wine was 2005. They had climatic challenges like the rest of the wine world. In spite of the frost damage at this Grenache site, Michael and Matt reiterated their excitement for the forthcoming quality of 2010. Having worked an excellent year and a horrible one in the recent past, I was feeling blessed to be here for this one.

Once the scenic side of the morning came to an end, we were ushered off to the grim reality of Branson for "an easy day" according to Matt. Chelsea and I were assigned "barrel room maintenance" by Ben, who was laughing as he handed us the gear to do it. The words "barrel room" make it easy to envision a picturesque wine cave or state of the art stainless steel, cool, humidified haven where only the finest French oak barrels were stacked for proper aging. Branson's barrel room was just a large, foam insulated, corrugated slab of concrete with no fans, cooling capabilities or anything else. It was empty at the moment, but as harvest would pick up, all the wines we'd make at this facility would go into barrels and age through the winter here, before being moved to either Rocland or the Marananga winery once summer warmed up. This routine allowed the vermin to feast on the insulation all summer long, and it was our job to eradicate the dead rats and patch up the chewed pockets in the walls. I had a chisel and a broom, and one by one I knocked each caked-to-the-concrete carcass loose and swept it into an industrial trash bag. Chelsea made it clear from the get-go that her contribution would be taping the insulation up.

After a half hour of this, Ben came down to check on us and said, "You can never wash the Branson outta ya, mate."

She carried on with patching up of foam and tape, using a ladder to get to the higher sections of the wall, and leaving me to handle the furry deceased. After awhile I got used to it, but the smell was horrendous.

Timmy was handed the nastiest job of us all, which was pressure washing the fermentation tanks up in the still active birdhouse, which we were elegantly calling "the aviary." They should've called in a Haz-Mat team for this. So much for all the safety precautions and hi-visibility shit: Timmy needed an astronaut suit on in the midst of the salmonella sludge. The kid roughed it out though, burning himself on the leaky, scorching pressure washer rifle, shoveling out two new dead birds, dodging their aggravated, frazzled swoops as he was blasting away. Once the slime had all been shot down below into an ultimately shit and feather-clogged drain, he scooped the liquid fecal mounds out with his bare, ungloved hands, then went and ate his lunch.

We finished up the day on a much higher note back at Marananga, with an oak comparison tasting put together by Michael and Matt. We tasted through mostly 2009 Shiraz wines that were aged in either new or old oak barrels, and we wrote down our rankings of the samples for their research purposes. I detected woody flavors in all of the wines, but good ones, since Two Hands was using the best barrels you could buy. Once revealed, my favorites were wines aged in either brand new barrels or one-year-old barrels. The sweetness of the wood lifted up these purple, fruit loaded wines to an extra dimension. I could see why critics would give these wines high scores in a room full of other samples to taste. At the end, we tasted the "Fly by Nighters" Vintage Port just to get the weekend started. Michael announced that harvest was hitting early this year, and that this was likely to be our last full weekend off together before things got full on.

"So go out and get shit-faced this weekend. We want stories on Monday." He pointed out that, after what we'd seen today in the vineyards, we could be done with fruit intake by Easter, which was at the beginning of April. So much for a mellow February to ease into things.

Timmy and I packed up our shack in Eden Valley and left a note for Aaron and Steff with $50 each laying on it. I thought it'd be best if we got out of there jail-break style, in the event that Greg's disappearance in the night soured their view of foreigners completely. We happily moved into "the derailment" in the warm early evening, and I called first priority on the big bed. The twin sized bed was connected to it and, while talking about the set up earlier in the day with Matt (who personally loaned Timmy the money to move in), he suggested we switch it up every week when the motel staff clean the room. We crammed our groceries into the honor bar sized fridge and the cabinets above, and I chilled a bottle of O'Leary Walker Watervale Riesling. I was going to cook up something good if the woman named Lynn at the front desk would grant me kitchen privileges. I asked her nicely, and she said if I kept it quick and clean, "then no dramas mate." I smoked part of a joint on the train porch for inspiration, then trotted over my core ingredients for the chicken schnitzel fettuccine alfredo. Turned out Lynn was Chris's mom. It was Friday night happy hour in their little lounge, with some old folks sitting around the bar for the cheaper pints of beer. As I started prepping in the back, she came over.

"Let's keep this quiet and not regular. We can't have the other backpackers all in here doing this," she said. I took that as my cue to make her a plate. I got back to the train car, or what we were referring to as the "choo-choo," in time to see Timmy scrapping the last of his cereal and milk for dinner. Feeling generous, but mainly high, I shared a plate with him. The orange light of the early evening shone on the vineyard just outside the train windows. I twisted off the Riesling and poured a solitary glass, and the grom stood up, grabbed a wineglass, and set it out in front of me, frothing for it.

I poured him a half glass. The wine was bright and clear in appearance, with cool citrus and gasoline notes. This Clare Valley stuff seemed to whiten your teeth and sanitize your mouth as it went down.

Over dinner he showed me the scar where they removed most of his liver when he was ten. "That's why I don't drink much," he said, drinking down every drop of what I poured him.

* * *

Gareth, Timmy, Calie and I day tripped two hours south to McLaren Vale in Gareth's car on Saturday. I brought along my baritone ukulele at Gareth's request, and played till the strings frayed. Gareth was from New Zealand and liked a lot of the same songwriters I did. Watching him work that week around the winery and listening to his comments during the few tastings we'd had as a team, it was clear that he was at an advanced wine level, and having already been through a harvest at Two Hands in 2008, he became the receptor of all of our annoying questions about how things were going to go. Our first stop was the bakery in the namesake township. I picked up a vegetarian pasty that was dusted in white and black pepper with a salted, buttery crust. I walked along the strip looking for a place to buy some sunblock and caught a windowsill of a small shop with esoteric French bottles on display. There was a dark haired woman in the alleyway unloading shippers of wine into the backdoor. "Hi love," she called out to me. I walked over and we started talking about wines straight away.

"Ah you're from the states are ya? Which part?" she asked.

"California."

Her eyes brightened. "Oh I love SF! I'm Gill."

"Hey Gill. I'm Darren."

The colorful conversation ranged from Berkeley-based Kermit Lynch wine imports, biodynamic wines, the wine bar Terroir on Folsom street, restaurants in the city, then we went into her tiny shop where I admired the bottles of wine. She'd started importing wines to Australia fairly recently to diversify the wine valley with old world opportunities. She was on a Gamay kick of sorts, and I recognized some labels from the Kermit Lynch book back home. The wines were marked up considerably high. I felt like buying one of the Cotes du Rhone Villages wines she had in there but couldn't justify the bottle cost. The other guys found me in there, and I introduced them to her. "I close at 3:30 and will be having a drink at Alpha, Box and Dice with Justin. Make sure to go there."

"I know the place," Gareth confirmed.

Our first winery stop was Oliver's Taranga, an operation that made a little wine for their own label but mainly supplied grapes to large wineries like Penfolds. A friendly pregnant woman was working the cellar door and poured us the wines with enthusiasm. The Fiano was a refreshing starting point, but their *Winestate Magazine* 5 star scoring Shiraz was an oxidized letdown. The Reserve Shiraz was decent, but not 45 dollars a bottle decent. My favorite wine was their Fortified Grenache named "The Banished," with black and white photo packaging and an outlaw story about the property to go along with it. Ben and his fiancée Megan showed up mid-tasting. She was finishing university in Adelaide and lived in the city with her folks, while Ben lived with his parents in the Barossa where he was born. Eventually they said they'd both live in the Barossa, as Ben saw a future with Two Hands. With short black hair and literary lenses, Megan was shy at first around us, but was kind enough to laugh at my stupid joke or two. We left without buying anything.

"Man, do you think she was chapped that we didn't buy?" I asked Ben outside.

He laughed and said, "No. You can walk in and walk right out and they don't mind."

"That's certainly different than back home," I pointed out. "If you taste and don't buy they talk smack about you when you leave."

Samuel's Gorge Winery was the next stop. We were taking Gareth's and Ben's suggestions for the itinerary. We crested a beautiful hilltop and drove to the left past an outdoor nature preserve of sorts, with turquoise ocean views to the west and open hillsides to the east. It was beautiful up here. Two slightly buzzed hippy girls were working the indoor tasting bar that housed an industrial espresso machine. I'd never seen that before in a tasting room and raved about how functional it was for the wine tasting experience. We were soon seated outside at small tables with a slight breeze and that view, and started off with a great Tasmanian Riesling, then onto a rich estate grown Tempranillo that Calie loved. Calie was maybe only 20 years old, and hailed from a family that owned vineyards in South Africa. His first language was Afrikaans, which I didn't even know was a thing. His family had urged him to do this harvest with Two Hands to gain winemaking experience, as they were planning on transitioning from simply being grape growers to making some of their own wine as a business. A mellow, semi-dirty Shiraz rounded out the lineup. Being another scorcher of a day, we arranged to come back at closing time to pick up some purchased bottles, and had complimentary, hand-pulled shots of espresso before heading to the next place.

We made it to Kay Brothers next which was loaded down with history and epic black and white photographs on the walls. The guy working there was really cool. We used to carry their Amery Cabernet at my mother's restaurant, and once I mentioned that, he made sure that we got to try their flagship wine called Block 6. The others didn't care too much for the place, saying it was a bit too dirty.

Ben reluctantly gave in on my request to go to D'Arenberg Winery. By him prefacing the place with "their wines suck big balls," I didn't expect too much heading in. The grounds were packed. There was a wedding going on, a bustling restaurant, and folks spilling out of the cellar door. Inside we found a list that featured over 30 current releases to try. I think they had almost every single grape varietal in bottle. You could get annihilated at this place if that's what you were after, and for free. I remember a wine called "The Wild Pixie" being my favorite, which was a Shiraz/Roussanne blend with a Ben and Jerry's Ice Cream-like label. It was a small dream come true to visit the place that made those wines I saved up for back in the day.

The final stop of the day was at Alpha Box and Dice. The small rectangular building on a gravel lot had graffiti on it, with pinball machines and some vintage thrift store furniture inside to lounge on. We met the owner Justin who was about my age and wearing a brown hat, t-shirt, and board shorts and pouring wines for folks from behind the tasting bar. He got out glasses for us while his blonde wife hand-labeled bottles of wine behind the counter and kept a light watch on their three kids that roamed about. The baby of the bunch stumbled around naked while we tasted a Dolcetto called "Dead Winemaker's Society." He wobbled up to an empty case box and started flapping at it. There just happened to be a huge huntsman spider on the box. His older brother came over and kicked the box. Justin broke story to say, "Hey now, don't do that, you're going to get bit." The bottles had original labels of edgy artwork on them, and the room itself was rootsy, with some funk, a beat down ghetto blaster on the ground playing tunes, and a vintage espresso machine behind the bar. These Australian tasting rooms know how to operate. "The Blood of Jupiter" Sangiovese/Cabernet almost had me reaching for the wallet, but "The Apostle" Shiraz/Durif was the clear standout. Justin mentioned how little wine he made, with everything being hand bottled. I purchased three bottles.

Gill from the wine shop turned up with a bottle of French Trousseau Gris that she had mentioned earlier. She poured tastes for us all. Justin decanted a 2004 Shiraz he made under his former label that was as fresh and dark as a brand new wine. He said he was planning on re-releasing a small amount of it in April, and to come back then. I had about two glasses of that stuff, and Ben raised an eyebrow at my drinking efforts. "Gareth's driving man," I pointed out. Ben was critical of every wine we tried during the day, but confessed to liking that 2004 too.

We made it back to Samuel's Gorge to buy some Riesling, then we followed Ben and Megan into Adelaide. The plan was to head to a wine shop he was raving about and have dinner in Chinatown at a place called Ying Chao that allowed BYOB. East End Cellars was a modern, well-lit wine shop near a complex of lofts and offices, loaded with curated bottles familiar and foreign, and we were hitting the aisles and examining labels immediately. Two guys Ben knew were working behind the check out area at the front of the store. I picked up an Adelaide Hills Nebbiolo Rosé.

Gareth, Calie and Timmy were looking around too, but had been claiming to be short on money all day. I figured with six of us headed to dinner, that a bottle each contribution would be fair. Timmy was walking around the store with a bottle. "Is that the one you're bringing tonight?" I asked.

He looked at me. "I think so. I don't really have any money. We should bag all the wines and do them blind though." He looked at Ben and said, "Blind tasting is the only real way to taste I think."

I held up my rosé. "Just a hunch but I'm pretty sure we'd be able to pick this one out tonight."

I asked Ben's opinion on a hand-labeled red blend from the Adelaide Hills that claimed no electricity was used in the production of the wine. Domaine Lucci was the name on the label. I picked it up anyhow for $28, along with a Heathcote Shiraz and the rosé that Ben told me was made by our grower Tom Shobbrook. Ben was preaching the Adelaide Hills as being one of the more exciting areas for wine in Australia these days, being more cool climate than Barossa which catered to lower alcohol levels and more natural acids in the fruit.

When all was said and done, Ben and I were the only two people at the register. Ben looked around and called out Gareth. "I probably won't drink man. I've gotta drive back." Fair enough.

"Guess it's just us then," I said to Ben. I paid $91 and we took the wines to the car.

Megan had gotten a call back from Ying Chao saying they were booked solid. It was Chinese New Year's and here we were in Chinatown in a city of 1.1 million. Grabbing a table was going to be iffy. We parked and roamed the crowded streets, looking for places to eat. The quickest spot to get in was called Barbecue City, and soon we were seated at a round table in the middle of the tiny dining room.

Ben brought his own stemware, and we got the bottles going. I opened my Domaine Lucci blend, and Ben uncorked a Luke Lambert Shiraz from the Yarra Valley. We started with mine, and it poured cloudy red with some effervescence. No one at the table cared for it. Timmy started verbally attacking it, which I found rather ironic in his non-contributing state of being. Megan and Ben handled the food ordering. We moved on to Ben's wine, which in sleek appearance alone was a big step up in quality.

This was probably the best Shiraz I'd had in Australia so far. Cool climate pepper scents, beef, and with richness and length on the finish. Timmy kept helping himself to that wine—the good one—until he poured all over the table.

After dinner, we picked up Kim from a restaurant across the way with Chelsea and her boyfriend James. We all crammed into Gareth's car and took the long drive back to Barossa. I started jamming on the uke in the backseat and Timmy started freestyling some rhymes, with topical subjects such as beast masters, Shiraz and cougars. We would've stayed and drank in the late night-lights of the city if some of these people actually had a little money.

* * *

The next morning saw our train car under attack by the local ant population. Should've known better than to leave the dirty chicken alfredo plates out in the bathroom sink for two days. Timmy got the brunt of it in the morning. He took the dirty plates back to the restaurant before driving to the Nuriootpa public library parking lot to score free Wi-Fi. As I killed the remaining trail of them on the table by the microwave, I started to see the necessary functionality of kitchenettes in weekly rental situations. Our choo-choo might not have been such a dream. The only sink was in the small bathroom—hardly the spot to wash or store dishes. I brewed up some of the Flying Goat coffee I had brought and got online for awhile, before opting to walk up into Nuriootpa for some lunch and groceries.

After 30 minutes of walking besides vineyards and the Penfolds Winery itself, I made it to the Branch Café and was presented with a menu full of salads, sandwiches and artisan pizzas. I ordered a sandwich and a rosé called "Three Dickie Birds." I shopped in the adjacent grocery store and made the walk back, only to find a red Magna parked by itself in the library parking lot, with a kid in headphones sitting in the passenger seat using the complimentary internet.

CHAPTER 9

We had our mandatory confined space training in Marananga on Monday. Since we'd soon be inside the tanks we had been cleaning the previous week, shoveling out gassy grape skins for pressing, all of the cellar casuals had to get certified to do so. There was plenty of work to do in the winery, but this was a crucial part of Australia's safety regulations. A thick, classic old Aussie safety trainer led the seminar in the upstairs office at Two Hands. A lifetime of smoking and television watching exuded from the look and sound of him. The kind of guy you'd want to publicly do a reading of any part of *Lord of the Rings*. I was first to try on the safety harness that wraps up hard inside the crotch. "I haven't worn one of these since Valentine's Day," I said.

"I don't wanna hear what ya did with that mate," the instructor joked. He asked if any of us were claustrophobic and I admitted I was. He gave me a double take, as if I was trying to get another laugh, but I wasn't. "You *do* know that you'll be wearing an oxygen mask and tank as part of your curriculum today, don't ya?"

"Yeah. I'm not excited about it, but yeah."

My mother was claustrophobic, and a few minor but key events in my life had made me follow in her footsteps. I was locked inside a walk-in refrigerator at the steakhouse in Eureka by the owner's prankster son, and once at a neighbor's house was dared to crawl into this odd coffin like compartment in the wood base of his bed when my brother and the neighbor closed it shut on me. I still vividly remember that one with a tremble to this day.

All my joking turned to sweaty, trembling tension as we all conducted the exercise. I was tapping my boot like I was at a Bakersfield honky tonk, and was last in line. "Guess who's next?" the instructor goaded me. I was shaking, red in the face and fumbling with setting up the tank and mask from the get-go. I put on the industrial mask, opened up the airflow, then everything went white. The instructor got up off his fat rump and helped me tighten the flaps on my mask. I've never been one for scuba diving, snorkeling or anything along those lines, and here I was the eldest of the Two Hands Vintage casuals, freaking the fuck out in front of everyone.

Once the oxygen was on, it was strange and difficult to breathe. I didn't trust it. Timmy quickly drew a cartoonish, wide-eyed portrait of me in the mask with a panicked expression on my face. The main part of the demonstration involved cutting off your own airflow so the instructor could check the negative pressure on your mask and the tank, to see if you kept calm for ten seconds or so. As I suffered through it, instead of closing the valve, I kept spinning it open, blasting excess oxygen in my face. He okayed me once I shut it off and tried not to pass out, while I did the final stretch of walking down the office stairs and back up, breathing through the mask while the world closed in on me. At the end, I ripped it all off my head and turned off the oxygen too fast, making a wild squealing sound. My coworkers laughed. "Take it easy there, mate," the instructor said, disturbed himself by my sweaty, frazzled response to the whole exercise. I had passed like everyone else, though as he signed my certificate, he said "You may want to delegate interior tank work during vintage, whenever possible."

After work that day, Timmy, Ben and I went to the local bottle shop to look around and grab some wines. This place had an unreal array of Australian icons in glass cases, and a huge selection of South Oz wines in temperature controlled conditions. I bought a Spinifex "Esprit" from the shop, which I'd never heard of, but judging from the blend of Mataro, Grenache, Shiraz and Cinsault, it looked like this small local producer had a French inspired style, with a listed alcohol of 14.0% which was low for around here. Ben was impressed when he saw the bottle in my hands. "Those wines are good, mate," he said with a six-pack of Coopers Pale Ale in hand.

With the train car being pretty size limited for sociability, and Ben still living with his parents, we took our purchases down to the house Nathan was renting on Murray Street. It was so close that we left Timmy's Magna in the little parking lot at Tanunda Cellars and walked there. Kim and Calie were renting out the other two rooms in the spacious, single-level house that had a large front and backyard. Timmy and I knew immediately, once stepping inside, that we got absolutely screwed on the accommodations. This was a real house, with real house things, like a kitchen sink, a backyard, a couch, and a refrigerator. He demanded to know how much Kim was paying as we walked through the door. We drank through the beers, and I was getting the drift that Kim was perhaps already coupled up with Nathan, the way she relaxingly sat sidekick on the couch with him and flirted with the tall ginger cellar hand. We ordered take away pizza from a shop up the street, which proved to incite all out heartburn hell in the company of the spicy Spinifex. It was a hot early evening to begin with, and the wine warmed up to accentuate the alcohol and spice, just by sitting on the kitchen counter and in our glasses. Close to nine, Timmy said he wanted to get going. "Where's your car?" Nathan asked.

"It's parked at the wine shop. In the lot," he said.

"They close that lot off," Nathan said with a laugh. "You should go have a look."

Timmy and I walked off only to find his red car trapped by the little chain on the posts around the driveway. There was no way around it. He was snapping. It was confusing and funny at the same time. It wasn't a gate — just a chain, and with the Magna being near low rider status anyway, I was convinced Timmy could slink right under it if I held it up. He pulled up to me as I held it to give it a try, but the chain snagged the windshield.

"Man, I bet if we lube the windshield we can easily get it out," I said. "Like with olive oil or dish soap or something."

"No way."

"Seriously, it's right there." Part of me was amused about the possibility of just driving through the fucking thing and tearing off down the street. It was Australia, the wild West, and being a liquor store that closed obscenely early like this one, I figured people would understand. It could possibly build upon our legends. Timmy was against it though, so we stumbled back defeated and asked if we could crash on Nathan's couches.

CHAPTER 10

I had been digging a ditch in the hot red dirt all day behind the Marananga winery with Timmy, until Timmy drove the pick ax into the fire emergency water tank line. In the lab during a break afterward, I finally received my visa nomination approval. "You can stay in the country mate," Matt Wenk said with the printout in his hands. Shadowing us was the new guy Michael Rizzo who hailed from Napa Valley most recently, but had a flamboyant East Coast accent. He was older than me, black bearded with tiny circular spectacles, and said he was here to have some fun drinking the fruity bombshells of the Barossa. Sadly, with the earlier than expected flow of the harvest, he was thrown right into it, missing the rib lunch and McLaren Vale weekend. It had cost him over five hundred bucks to change his flight, since he'd heard about my tough entry and chose to wait until his work visa was finalized. It was sweltering hot, temperatures cranking all day and night, and the vineyards were ripening fast for the crushing.

After getting my official visa from Matt in the break room, he sent me over to Rocland in a company truck to finish the afternoon with Heintje. It was my first time at Rocland, and it was as big of a factory as I imagined. Just driving the loop in past the massive outdoor tanks I could see why a guy like Greg couldn't fathom putting in three months straight of his life there. Two Hands leased the far building for barrel and case goods storage. I shared a tight spot on the scissor lift with Heintje, rising up six barrels high to collect vials of wine. We were getting samples from the reserve tier of wines that were soon to be analyzed and bottled after Michael Twelftree and Matt tasted through them. They were supposed to bottle these wines before harvest to make space for the new crop, but they put it off for some reason. I asked Heintje what he thought of these wines.

"I don't mind new oak when it's balanced with fruit and acid," he said. We were mainly pulling Aerope Grenache and Ares Shiraz samples from the hogsheads. Every sample smelled powerful and delicious. He was open to answering my questions, often replying in sarcastic brevity, and always with the nervous snorting laugh. I was mainly wondering about the 12-hour days that were mentioned in our contract, and when they would start. I asked him if Richard Mintz, the other owner and "hand" that we hadn't met yet, would be there along with us putting in 12-hour days as well.

"Twelve holes maybe," he replied with a gust from the septum.

There was a human resources drama between Ben and Heintje. Heintje, with his shaved head, gold hoop earrings and plump smooth face that made you want to eat a pasty on sight, wanted the assistant winemaker position that became available when the former assistant hastily took a position with Henschke in Eden Valley. Since Ben had put in two previous vintages at Two Hands and had a degree from the University of Adelaide, he secured the spot weeks before we turned up. Heintje pointed out to me on the scissor lift that he was looking for an alternative job post vintage. He was a strange cat, encouraging water cooler talk on the job, but also timid at times with worried eyes always looking out for superiors. He rode a motorcycle and wore a black astronaut-like biker suit and helmet to and from work. He seemed okay to me, even though Ben and even Nathan bad talked him a bit. As our winemaker Matt often said about trippy people in the Valley, "It takes all kinds."

* * *

After work I sat alone in the derailed train carriage dusting a bottle of Winter Creek "Second Eleven" Shiraz-Grenache, smoking hydro, and chatting online with a 21-year-old girl in Sonoma who didn't really like me all that much. Timmy was off at the Branson facility, brown-nosing Matt by helping off the clock with the bottling of Matt's own private label of wines called "Smidge." I was getting the drift that Timmy wasn't handling the off time well here on this anthill in a haunted train car. Or maybe I'm a terrifying portrait of older humanity. I drank the last of the soft, chocolaty Winter Creek with pan-fried lamb steaks and mashed potatoes, then watched the panoramic pink of the sunset turn purple in the west as the mosquitoes drove their fangs into my American flesh.

The rumbling engine of Timmy's Magna came around a bit later, and he strolled in more buzzed than I was somehow, with a smirk to tell me about the nice dinner Matt treated him to for helping with the Smidge wines.

"How'd that go?" I asked.

He stopped, arranging some things on his little bed, and said "Matt is intense. I'm probably not going to volunteer to help with that anymore. He kinda goes off."

"Like a yeller?"

"Oh yeah," he said

I had a dream that night where I was waiting tables at my mom's restaurant in California. I had a table that wanted a straw basket flask of Chianti, but I upsold them to a bottle of Foxen Sea Smoke Vineyard Pinot Noir that was on the list for $120. Excited about that, I charged into the office to where my mom was sitting, as usual, doing paperwork and spacing out over piles of old mail and magazines, and told her the good news. I looked around the storage area for the pricey bottle while she stood behind me, and I realized she had taken the whole case home. I started yelling at her, right in her face. I walked away, went through the kitchen, and saw that the prep cook load from the day before was only half-finished: non-portioned spaghetti, a tray of lasagna missing its top layer, just chaos. The restaurant had just opened, and it was then that I realized that I was supposed to be waiting tables at my father's restaurant clear across the county, not at my mom's place. I didn't call him to let him know, I just got in my truck with my apron on and was driving around a big foreign city pissed off and honking the horn.

CHAPTER 11

Running about two weeks early for the norm, we received a decent load of McLaren Vale Shiraz at Branson. Everywhere I'd worked in the past, the grapes would arrive in white, square-like macro bins that held a half ton in each. At Branson, the fruit arrived in the back of an industrial dump truck, the bed of which was filled with machine harvested little black clusters with green stems. The crushing area was unlike anything I'd ever seen. It had a gravity advantage to the process, so that the trucks could drive up from behind the aviary building, back in to the edge above the crush pad, right above the massive steel hopper and scale, and open up the rear gate and raise the load to all come gushing down in one big purple swoosh. I'd never seen anything like it. The truckers would take off right afterward without even hosing out the trucks. This was big business.

Nathan was down below checking the weight of the delivery before firing up the destemmer. The destemmer had a hand control to monitor the flow of destemmed grapes that were pumping through the crusher and down the hose toward a tank. There was water in the hose ahead of the fruit, so Calie was inside the small tank room holding the end of the hose off the side of the tank. He was ready to "catch" the wine, meaning once he saw purple coming out he'd stuff the hose into the sanitized and ready tank. Nathan had me head up above the hopper on the catwalk with another remote control, guiding me through operating the big hopper that was slowly pushing the fruit down to the destemmer. It was a three-person gig to run smoothly, but I imagined that soon it'd be a one-person show. I was excited to see this real first day of the wine harvest happening, and the view from the catwalk above the hopper in mid day sunlight was phenomenal, with the fruit bearing vines of Branson Coach House Vineyard surrounding me and the low, dry, open hills of the Barossa stretching out beneath the skies.

At dinner, which consisted of pizzas at Branson in the lingering heat of the day, Matt asked the group who would like to have the next day off, since harvest was going to start raging and things were going to get full on. Being somewhat seasoned, I raised my hand immediately, not looking to be the hero here. This was life. Hirsch Vineyards taught me to take a free day if and when available no matter what, and to stay gone on that entire day. Everyone else denied the offer, so Matt granted me the day off. There wasn't supposed to be any fruit coming in to be processed, and it was allegedly going to be an easy Friday. I was smart enough to know that you never know.

That night, Timmy and I hosted the first party of the season in our train car. We told Kim and the crew to bring bathing suits for the pool, which was turning out to be the only desired luxury of our spot. I was using it nightly for exercise and surely hairline reduction with its noxious parts per million of chlorination. Ten people showed up right on time and we packed into the choo-choo, drinking through Ben's six pack of Coopers, and an array of wines, plus an expensive 2007 "The Little Grenache" from an allegedly "lunar" biodynamic-minded woman winemaker in Marananga, whose winery Matt had pointed out on our vineyard tour. Matt claimed she did all nude *pigeage*. We had a string of laughs going while Ben, Gareth and I stood around assessing the wine. "One hundred percent whole bush fermentation," I declared.

"Lifted hood," Ben added.

"Lifted labia notes, maybe some vanillin vagina," I concluded.

When we had a collective buzz, we sat outside around our carriage door, and Kim dropped some emotional blues on us out of nowhere about her father's early recent death, which confused us all. I cringed because earlier that day, while Kim and I were filling up a wine tank for transport with a friendly trucker, Kim had mentioned being among a family of three wild daughters, and I made the light, silence-filling joke in front of the trucker of "Man, is your dad even alive still?" She had said no, but I wasn't sure if that was a joke or not. It apparently wasn't, and it took condolences and me breaking out my harmonica and ukulele to get the party going again. "I'm sorry, I just wanted to let you guys know, okay," she said a couple times later with a slur.

"Let's go to the pool," she said to me a short while later.

"The grotto?" I joked. Timmy and I had been giving the pool some serious Playboy mansion luster all day, even though it was everything but. "All right," I said, standing up. "Does anyone else wanna go?"

It was late, and work was due to begin at seven for them. I had the day off, however, and she and I walked over toward the indoor recreation area. Most of the other train cars were empty. I lit a joint and her eyes glowed along with the orange tip. "What is that?"

"It's a joint. Here."

"Really? How did you find it so fast over here?"

"Oh I go insane if I don't have it. Nearly first priority. Here. Go ahead."

We passed it back and forth, coughing to break up the silence, and I put it out before unlocking the pool house door and going inside. We were the only ones there, and the lights were off at nine as per the house rules. She stripped down to an all-black utility swimsuit and jumped in. I followed and treaded water in the warmth of the deep end. We were at opposite ends of the pool. Small talk followed for a moment, before we found ourselves treading water inches away from each other, mouths close. I could have easily started kissing her but I resisted, and left the opportunity open to her. She came in closer and then all of a sudden shivered audibly and said "I just got so cold. I'm-I'm freezing." She swam away, leaving me to tread by myself for a few more moments before climbing out and toweling off, my eyes burning.

"I can't miss my ride," she said, as Ben was supposed to drive her to Nathan's house in Tanunda.

The train car party was in full swing when we got back, with people drinking and laughing inside and out. I fished through our honor bar of a refrigerator for a bottle of Torbreck Mataro rosé, olives and Mersey Valley vintage cheddar. Kim just sat there on the edge of the bed, glossy eyed and silent, waiting for us to finish up drinking so she could get her ride from Ben.

"Does Barossa Bandol exist?" I asked Ben, drinking the stellar rosé.

"It might mate."

* * *

I awoke to the sound of Timmy chomping through at least three bowls of cereal, which was the only food to his name. Breakfast, lunch *and* dinner, it was cereal. It sounded like a horse at the trough. I got up, brewed water for coffee in the kettle, and started hot rinsing leftover glassware and a cheesy knife. It was close to eight.

"I guess we're getting fruit today," Timmy said to me. "I just got a call from Ben."

"Fuck, I'm outta here," I said. Two Hands wasn't supposed to get any grapes, hence my day off. I knew this game, so I took off on foot toward town, put the Carter Family on through my headphones, and cruised down Murray Street toward Tanunda. I wore sandals, brown corduroy pants, a flannel, shades, and a fedora hat. I was smiling, walking in the morning heat, the day free, when a red work truck with "Stevens Electric" on its doors drove towards me and I locked eyes with the driver who started flipping me off passionately, with these wild up and down thrusts of his wrists. He kept on driving. My whole bluegrass vibe screeched to a halt, but then I started laughing. It was a workday in a workingman's town, and I did look like a bohemian, which I would learn over the course of the vintage is akin to being bigfoot, or the Loch Ness monster in Barossa.

I found the Tanunda Music Centre by the Foodland in town and browsed through the guitar and amplifier section of the store. The owner offered tentative help and I told him I was here for strings and to have a look. They had a guitjo in there for $450, and a Gibson SG like the one I had at home for $2,000. While going through the strings selection the owner started talking about playing music. I asked if he knew of the Yearlings.

"Yeah, they're friends of mine."

"I played a show with them at the Wheatsheaf when I first got here." He looked at me in great distrust.

"Oh yeah?"

"Yeah, it was cool. I got to hear some of the new stuff they recorded on eight track with Mick. Do you know him too?"

"Um..."

"Mixmasters Studio."

"Yeah I know of him."

We started talking a little about vintage instruments and he clarified that Robyn's Gibson I was able to play at the show was a J-45. "There are heaps of vintage instruments in Barossa," he said, citing the German heritage in the area. He told me that he and his wife formed a booking company and started giving gigs away because they got so many private functions at the wineries.

"Where do you book at?" I asked him.

"We booked the Yearlings' show at the Regional Gallery here. That's end of March. But mainly at The Branch in Nuri."

"How long of a set is that? Two hours?"

He smiled and said "Nah four. Usually the performer does four forty five minute sets. Sometimes we'll have people split the gig. It's wallpaper music really. Each person doing two hours."

"Can I write down my music site for you to check out. I'd love to play somewhere if you're interested."

"Sure, how long're you here for?"

"Through April. Then I'm going do head down to record some stuff with Mick."

"What do you play?"

"Acoustic stuff, with harmonicas. I do originals and covers."

"What kind of covers?"

"Oh Dylan, Kristofferson, the Dead, stuff like that."

"Yeah write it down and I'll have a listen." I jotted down the link for him. "I'll just have a listen first and then I'll email you."

"Sounds good." I paid for my strings and picks and finally introduced myself with an outstretched hand. "I'm Darren."

"I'm Jamie," he said. The whole exchange was cautious on his part till I tried to leave. Then he kept talking as I was walking away. "We have tickets for The Yearlings show here if you want to buy one."

"I'll have to make sure Two Hands gives me the day off first," I said.

"Well, I'll have a listen to your stuff right now. We're always looking for new people."

I had a coffee at Kiel's, wrote in my journal, and then checked out the two galleries in town, smoking a joint in between.

That night when Timmy got off, I had polished off the rest of the Torbreck Saignée. He was fired up to go out to either of the two local bars, and showered up and put on nice clothes. We went to the Clubhouse and found the only women to be 16-year-olds drinking soda and playing pool. We drank Coopers and waited for a pool table to open up. Some obnoxious harvest hands from South Africa were hogging up one table, and the grommet girls had the other. The guys were pouring money into the expensive electro jukebox, playing classic rock jams and making progress with the local jezebels.

"This is depressing," I said to Timmy.

Going for a second ale, I thought about the fact that Barossa Valley has one of the highest suicide rates in Australia, and shared that newsflash with Timmy. "And this nearby town called Kapunda… guess it's one of the southern hemisphere's most haunted towns." They were small factoids to lube the disconcerting fact that we wouldn't be having sex in the Barossa Valley at this rate.

CHAPTER 12

The Branson facility had crushed a lot of Shiraz by the time Timmy and I arrived at 1 PM. Tempers were flaring and more unexpected grapes were on the way. Matt had just snapped on Calie regarding a bin tipping command on the forklift, which was enough to freak the young guy out. "Take it with a grain of salt mate," Ben told the confused, huffing and puffing Saffa when we walked up. Timmy jumped into hot rinsing one of the inside tanks for the next crush load, but left the bottom valve open, which led to close to a ton of Shiraz spewing out onto the dirty concrete. Ben and I noticed it while he was asking me about my day off, drinking coffee that I made in a small press. All of a sudden Nathan walked in to double check the tank and got absolutely blasted by juice spraying him through the open valve.

"Hwah!" Nathan shrieked. "Ben, think we should tell him to stop?"

"Stop!" Ben screamed, which was the command for shutting off the must pump.

I ran outside and shouted it again, because the crusher was across a few rows of big tanks and whoever was operating it didn't hear the first time. Ben marched Timmy in there to show him what happened like a dog. I started to pitch in to clean it up but Nathan stopped me. "That's Timmy's mess," he said. "He'll clean it up."

On the dry erase board above the small desk in there, it was written that on the following Monday we were getting 30 tons of Shiraz and four tons of Clare Valley Riesling. By Monday, if all went well, we would have already crushed 200 tons somehow, out of the 750 predicted. That would put us a third of the way into harvest and fill up most of our fermentation tanks. Because of the endless heat wave, Ben said 2010 would be one of the earliest harvests on record at Two Hands.

There was an anxiety-ridden energy going around about when all the real chaos was going to hit. When you are just crushing and fermenting at the start of harvest, the shifts are fairly easy to predict. But when you add pressing and barreling down to the mix, it takes real organization to keep things running upbeat and as smooth as possible. However, the vibe coming from Branson was already there, and I started to get irritated with Gareth even, who was the gentle, soft spoken shift supervisor. He had to pump over three of the big hanging potter tanks through the glycol lines to cool the temperature of the fermenting juice down, spending about 45 minutes to an hour on each of them. They were nearing 100 degrees, which could kill off the yeast population and leave you with half of a volatile dessert wine. The cooling system kept tripping itself off and he was calling out to me from up above in the aviary to check the mobile glycol chiller and reset it. I was pumping over tanks of my own and kept having to break to help him out. He was hard to hear and I had no idea how the chiller even worked. I even cursed him for caring too much at one point. My other coworker of the night was Michael Rizzo. I was excited to meet him initially and talk wine with a true connoisseur who'd worked at some serious wineries in Napa, but he was showing a side of him that was annoyingly flirty, raunchy with sexual innuendo, and on a mission to push mine and Gareth's buttons. I took a little break from him at one in the morning and sat in the dirty desk chair by myself and was yawning when he walked in and screamed at the top of his lungs *Wake up!* Shortly afterward I was squeegeeing up grapes around the destemmer from the night's processing and he walked over shouting, "Oh no! What did you do Darren?!" I was desperately trying to see the harmless humor and social rapport in that, but I couldn't. He was wearing an awful lot of Native American jewelry for being dressed in high-visibility work gear.

Gareth successfully chilled those big tanks down and, through all of the minor ups and downs, we closed down Branson at the thirteen-hour mark, dirty, wet and exhausted.

CHAPTER 13

While waiting to be picked up for work on Sunday afternoon, I sat out on the porch and played a few songs on my baritone ukulele. I noticed Chris and his brindle boxer Jill lurking on the backside of the railway. I couldn't tell if he was walking his dog or just checking the perimeter of his funky motel. I'd seen him walk by when I was strumming inside earlier. On the third pass I stopped and acknowledged him. He smiled sheepishly, standing there next to a drainage and a bird netted vineyard.

"You play the guitar!" he said.

"Yeah. It gives me peace of mind."

"Right. Say, have you got Fridays off?"

"Last week I did, this week I might. My friend Timmy has today off."

I thought we were just chatting about work, then he said, "Hey, if you're not working Friday, you should let me feed a few pints into ya, bring the guitar in for our happy hour."

"To play?"

"Sure mate, why not?"

"That'd be cool."

"Happy hour starts at five. Say come in, play six to eight. Whatever you want."

"I have harmonicas too."

"Have ya now?" He was smiling.

"Yeah. Well I'll find out from the winemaker what our schedule is and let ya know."

He mentioned that Timmy and I wouldn't have to temporarily move out that next weekend per his anticipated fully booked scenario for the "Day on the Green" concert that was approaching, starring Tom Jones.

"If you do have to move us for those days," I said to him, "can you put us closer to number thirty-one?" He got it immediately and his eyes twinkled.

"Ahh mate, the Jacob's Creek girls. Pretty nice, eh? Have you met them?"

"Yeah. In the pool one morning."

"Deal." His dog shot into our room like a Tasmanian devil. He shouted at her and she ran right back out.

"Well, I'll let ya know about playin'," I said.

Just then a brand new gold Toyota pulled up to the green train car Chris and his dog seemed to live in just across from ours. A blonde woman in a tight short skirt and high heels got out. I started Flamenco finger picking immediately for attention and she looked over. Jill ran over and the woman knew the dog by name. Chris walked over to her and soon they disappeared from the sunshine into his own residential train car.

I played a little more, thinking about the Sunday work scene ahead of me. Grapes were being crushed at the more posh and less verminated Marananga facility, but supposedly not much was happening at Branson. Matt pulled up in his Two Hands logo adorned Subaru, and he, Rizzo and I drove along toward the winery. I told Matt about the impending bookings and he was amused. "Big time, eh? We'll all come in and watch ya mate," he said, smiling, then he laughed.

Heintje was driving the forklift when we pulled up at Marananga. Kim and Nathan were on the morning Branson crew, where Michael and I were bound to work. They had a pump die out, with no service tech available till Monday, so we had to haul a spare pump over. Rizzo and I drove a truck over to Branson, and I put my headphones on and worked on the indoor, eight-ton capacity fermenter tanks, then did a round of pump overs. Once Shiraz started fermenting, the protocol at Two Hands was to pump each tank over three times throughout the course of 24 hours, thirty minutes at a time. If the juice was getting too hot, you either had to extend the pumpover an extra thirty minutes or connect the hose to the glycol chiller, which was a pain. It could seem monotonous, but if you liked to let your mind wander it was job stability.

Rizzo, Gareth, Matt and I had pizza for dinner before sunset. Then it was onto the big hanging ten ton potter tanks in the aviary. Six of the ten tanks were full of Shiraz, far earlier than in usual vintages around here, and some of them were nearing the point of pressing, which is when Matt said the bottleneck of vintage begins: having both grapes to crush and tanks to press on the same day. The tanks smelled so good, with intense purple color, and rich sweet flavors of the deepest, darkest berries, in spite of the amount of galactic snails and pigeon feathers imbedded in the uncovered caps.

Some of the fermentations, like in previous nights, were extremely hot before the pump overs were started. That was the routine: drop a thermometer in the thick, cap cake of skins to get a temp, then pull off a sample of wine in a cylinder to get a sugar reading. In the US this is called *brix*, but here is called *Baume*. Two of the tanks were nearing 40 degrees Celsius, which could cook the dwindling, tired yeast population, so I had to run the pumping wine through the glycol chiller like Gareth had. This entailed starting the pump over and tying the hose to the top of the tank, running down the three story flight of stairs to activate the cooling unit, then charging back up to control the pump and end of the hose. It was a good workout for sure and a break from the remaining nervous, fluttering pigeons who wondered what the hell happened to their home. I asked Gareth why these fermentations were getting so hot, and he attributed it to "the ambient temperature of Barossa."

Out of a plastic measuring cup, we were encouraged to taste the developing wines as they fermented and report on the pumpover clipboard if there were any problems. These unoaked, raw McLaren Vale Shiraz wines were some of the finest tank samples I'd tasted during a wine harvest, full of milk chocolate, boysenberry, pepper, and raw meat aromas. I was starting to believe what Michael and Matt were claiming about this vintage.

CHAPTER 14

Iorchestrated some considerable fuck ups at work the next day, including, but not limited to, starting pump overs upstairs with a pump that had been disconnected below from the must chiller. Ben caught it just in time with a loud angry *stop!* I stood on the third story catwalk looking down at him. "That could've been the fuck up of the vintage," he said. I got the drift that this guy wouldn't have minded seeing it happen for entertainment purposes. The lore of former cellar hand mistakes is rich at Two Hands. The Barossa thus far seemed like a pretty sleepy, lonesome desert of a place. To have some internationals come through for a couple months a year and set pumps on fire, sleep with each other, or drop ten tons of grapes on the filthy floor would fill up plenty of dead air till next time.

Heintje was there, cleaning up the bladder press for the incoming four ton lot of Riesling from Clare Valley for a wine Michael Twelftree called "The Wolf." The Clare Valley, being remotely located a couple hours north in a wooded, high elevation landscape, had as much of a reputation for Riesling as it did for weed.

"Where are those Clare Valley hippies at?" I asked Heintje.

"I don't know," he laughed with a nervous snort of the nostrils. "Maybe they stopped off for a cone."

It'd take me weeks to discover that a "cone" in South Australia speak is not ice cream. It's a joint. Which could lead to ice cream, which is why it's either brilliant or confusing.

By sunset we congregated at Marananga for our first dinner by the South African born harvest chef Eleni. She started things off with a curry and Matt opened up a couple Rieslings to go with it. Afterward, I rode back with him to Branson with confidence to do pump overs on what now had become eight full potter tanks. I walked up the stairway, high above the cycling bladder press that was finishing up the Riesling just below me. As per the routine of starting up pump overs, the hoses were full of water. Once the pump was turned on and you were hooked up to the bottom valve of the first wine tank, you had to push the water out of the line with wine, then rather than pump the water out from three stories up off the railing, you put the end of the exit hose into a custom PVC pipe that neatly funneled it down the stairway and out onto the cellar floor below. On this particular night, the water came blasting out into the drip pan below the press, with heavy potential to dilute the Riesling. I heard Matt yelling. He was snapping. I stopped the pump. Matt looked up and said, "Where is that water comin' from?!"

"I'm clearing the, uh, the line in the pipe," I said.

"Clear it out off the end mate. We're pressing down here!"

A couple days back he had rousted Ben a little for not clearing the line through the PVC pipe, saying "Use the pipe mate. That's what it's there for!"

I got to tank five, with its leaky bottom valve that the morning crew had warned us about. Imagine if that thing came off! With ten tons of suspended matter ready to gravity blast out of it! I connected the suction hose and delicately opened the valve. It immediately began to leak out black Shiraz. *Fuck*, I muttered to myself, grabbing the wrench and screwing it righty tighty. At the last second, I remembered that it was reverse around here. One wrong crank and not only would ten tons of Shiraz come pummeling down but the press below would become Pink Riesling. I called for Matt.

"This one's leaking," I said. He felt it and asked for something that was slang for the wrench. I handed it to him and watched as he tightened it lefty-loosey. He felt my other spots for tightness.

"Your clamps are all loose mate," he said, then he made a funny little wail when he looked down and saw purple leakage on the press below us.

"Oh no." I was freaked out.

"Nah nah, it's done mate," he assured me of the Riesling's press cycle.

With restored confidence, I excelled on the rest of the pump overs. Matt had forgotten to arrange for a trailer in the morning to haul the pressed little Riesling tank back over to Marananga for cold settling, so he borrowed a haggard, dusty trailer with an alleged half ton capacity from a silver bearded man down the road named "Father Christmas." He was an older man who made wine in ancient barrels and kept them outside all year round. Matt and I drove over late, and he arranged for a quick borrow of the thing. He latched it onto the back of the Two Hands truck and we drove back to Branson. The tank full of Riesling juice looked like R2D2 in *Star Wars*, and it easily weighed two and a half tons. I forklifted it onto the feeble, wood-rotted trailer and the thing audibly wheezed like a set of old lungs. Didn't phase Matt at all; he drove that bastard across Greenock and made it to Marananga that night, but couldn't get the tank off the trailer with the weaker forklift there. He soon called Heintje and I over from Branson to weigh down the back of the forklift, which didn't really work. "This is what vintage lunches are for," Heintje joked about his own weight. Even with our extra 400 pounds on the back, the rear tires of the forklift would pop up into the air when he tried to fork the tank off the trailer. After three more attempts he got it off the half warped trailer, but the forklift couldn't handle it. Heintje placed the orange pallet jack under one side of the tank to absorb some of the load and Matt lowered the tank onto it, which, after moving it inside the cellar to the spot where glycol cooling lines could be hooked up to it, completely bent the pallet jack out of commission.

"Yeah, maybe we shouldn't have done that," Heintje said with a snort. What mattered here was that the tank of Riesling had arrived as planned. Father Christmas on the other hand was gonna be chapped.

CHAPTER 15

The next evening I was upstairs doing pump overs when Ben turned up. It was his day off and his lips were blackened, carrying two bottles of wine and a glass. He walked them all the way up the infected metal perch to me. He had taken Gareth and Timmy to a tasting appointment with the winemakers at Standish Wine Company, and he brought the remains of a Shiraz, giving me a taste of their assistant winemaker's Shiraz fermented with stem inclusion. He was in generous spirits, and at this point of the monotonous routine, it was smart to be reminded of the good kind of wine we were slaving over.

When I got home Timmy was on his bed watching a movie on his laptop. There was an untouched six pack of Coopers Lager sitting warm on the table. He offered me one. I said thanks and put them away in the fridge, knowing some late night charcuterie and a half bottle of Standish was on my agenda. I logged into my computer and grabbed some stemware out of Ben's left-behind Spieglau box from the party, before putting together some prosciutto, olives, and Tasmanian cheddar curds to pair with what tasted silky and rich. It was hard to be classy and stylish in an odiferous, ant-infested train car, but I was trying. The combination of Kalamata olives, cured pork and Barossa Valley Shiraz eased my working man's pain and stirred my imagination. The Standish was the best Barossa Valley wine I'd had so far, and it had that magic dance of richness without heaviness that critic Robert Parker claims is the stuffing of outstanding wines.

With headphones on, Timmy eyeballed me with every sip. He wanted it. I poured my wine fast and loaded the glass up by the time the scrapper got out of bed to investigate my gastronomical scene. There were remnants of his go-to dinner of cold cereal on the table. I was listening to Little Dragon on my headphones as he came over and just picked up the bottle.

"Standish huh?" he said to me.

I pulled an earphone out. "What?"

"Standish?"

"Yeah."

"Hmm," he muttered, looking at the label closely again. "How much was it?"

"Hundred and twenty," I said all nonchalant. You could say I was egging the kid on. It stopped him in his tracks.

"One twenty? Can I smell it?"

"Sure."

He picked up my glass and stood there swirling. Wisely enough, he didn't dare sip it. My claws would have emerged. He went and brushed his teeth and got back into bed, not even opening up one of his beers. It had been odd lately, working these different shifts. I'd been getting home and he was still awake, but he seemed high, or drunk. I remembered the vicodin he was talking to Aaron about. Maybe he was one of those Malibu pill poppers.

I washed up the remains of my amateur tapas scene with motel bar soap and hot water, then got into bed. I had the big bed for only a couple more nights, then I'd be cramming myself into the crib-sized side bed that Timmy's been buckling down in. I had a dream that Kim and I started making out in an outdoor pool somewhere and that I immediately regretted it. That was followed by a dream that my non-drinking dad, brother and I were at a wine club event at Justin Winery's new tasting room which was in a hilly downtown developed block somewhere like Palo Alto. Fiji water bottles were everywhere, and Fiji water was even in barrels that were being sampled via wine thief by employees.

CHAPTER 16

The next day I memorized the song "Caroline" by Old Crow Medicine Show. On the baritone uke and with the C harp, the song sounded good enough to play at the derailment's happy hour. It was Friday after all. The days were flying by, and free time felt like mere seconds. Sleeping as long as possible was becoming the principal goal. I had to move mine and Timmy's things into train car #8 because of the Tom Jones concert coming into town and the whole motel getting booked out. Australian panties would fly this weekend.

That night, we had a delicious dinner from Eleni of pasta done two ways—carbonara or puttanesca. Both were beautifully arranged on platters and the right kind of comfort food our calorie burning bodies required. We went through the week's schedule, or roster if you will, in a peaceful enough sunset setting. I learned that I had the next Friday off, which would free me up to go to the World music festival on the day that my favorite band Calexico was playing. I'd have to borrow a car, take a bus, or hitchhike down there and back. "WOMAD's totally your scene," Nathan said to me at the table and laughed. Maybe I did look like a weed blazing hippy to everyone, not just blue collar randoms on Murray Street.

Matt was as social as I'd seen him, talking about surfing and hanging out while I did juice adds to the yeast. Creating the yeast to add to a tank of grapes was simple at Two Hands: forty degrees Celsius for the water, heated from a plastic water pitcher, then we'd add yeast and a little Shiraz juice, wait fifteen minutes, repeat two more times, then one last juice add to bring the pink frothy concoction within ten degrees of the tank temperature. I'd never worked at a winery where I had to do this. My previous harvest job at Hirsch relied solely on wild yeasts to start up and do the fermentation. This bakery-like process reminded me of making pizza dough at my mom's pizzeria, which I'd been making since I was fifteen years old. Relating the two processes, I soon got the hang of it.

I drank a rugged McLaren Vale Shiraz tank sample around 2:30 in the morning when we got off work. The wine was insane already. How could that be possible? It was crazy to taste the rich, purple, young fruit free of the weight of oak and sulfites. Pure brown sugar and bacon notes were bursting from the wine. The vibrant nectar put me out by about three in the morning.

CHAPTER 17

The big gossip around the winery when I returned for work was that Heintje allegedly spent the night with Kim. Chatter travels fast at Two Hands. Ben loved it the most, who spilled the rumor to me while we were barreling down McLaren Vale Shiraz. I asked Calie, who lived one room over from Kim, if he heard anything interesting last night.

"Yah," he smiled huge. "Like dogs. Wild dog noises."

We cracked up. We all didn't see that one coming. Heintje. The man who worked a random harvest at Rombauer and asked me if I knew what three shakes for $100 entailed at a strip club in SF called Crazy Horse. I didn't. The dancer took him in back and swiftly jacked him off.

"Tightass Timmy" was officially my roommate's new nickname around the winery too. He was reprimanded by Matt for his three plates full of dinner the other night, as well as his now infamous "curry sunrise" where he ate all the leftovers that were meant for the lunch break.

Michael Twelftree organized a lamb spit roast that evening at Marananga with an animal from the Kalleske Vineyard where Two Hands sourced high-end grapes. Michael coupled the feast with a single blind Syrah tasting featuring ten wines in the lab area. This meant that we saw the bottles of the wines, but they were switched up and poured into unlabeled glass bottles and numbered one to ten. He spared no expense, including a 1992 La Mouline from Guigal. My favorite wine ended up being the 2002 Greenock Creek Apricot Block Shiraz, no one else's. I got mixed up on the 2002 Owen Roe and the Hermitage, but I claimed eight of the ten wines to be what they were before being revealed. Ben called me a liar and demanded to see my notes. "I should come work for you, mate," Twelftree said at the table. We ate lamb Middle Eastern style with

Pita bread, hummus, and tabouleh and drank through our favorites. Sure we were starting to get hectic with the work schedule, with some 14-hour shifts going down, but this was a nice, spirit-lifting touch.

A few of us had the night off to go drinking in town, and I didn't get a chance to communicate with Timmy about our game plan before he left with our only room key. He was allegedly en route to the Clubhouse in Tanunda for beers. I asked Trent the vineyard manager for a lift into Tanunda. All of the casuals had recently learned that Trent was a professional drummer in various Adelaide bands. We talked about music on the drive over and surfing as well. He used to bodyboard down south quite a bit and said he'd be keen to go with me at some point. He dropped me off at the Clubhouse and left. I walked into the bright, older country club style barroom and found a few guys still wearing their high-visibility gear at the bar, while some teenagers played pool. No music was on, just the television sets. And worse, Timmy wasn't there.

I went to the Tanunda Hotel, the only other bar on the strip, and he wasn't there either. It was a thirty minute walk back to the train cars, but in between was the house that Chelsea, her boyfriend James, and some other Kiwis were renting for vintage. I turned up as they were finishing quite a few open bottles of wine and waited to be offered a glass. Without having a phone, getting around was proving to be difficult, even in Australia. Everyone was mainly talking about how much they'd been working, complaining about pay at the various wineries around the valley, and if it was a good year or not. I sat in a leather recliner and had a glass of Rusden, pretending to enjoy myself.

I ultimately did the rest of the walk back along Murray and found Timmy at the motel. He'd been there the whole time, on the internet, and not spending any money.

CHAPTER 18

I was assigned my big debut at the Marananga facility. After slaving away among the filth and pigeons of Branson, Kim and I crushed ten and a half tons of old vine Shiraz into the small rectangular steel tanks. She was an indefatigable, wise winery worker, and her sense of humor made her fun to be around.

I asked Kim about her last harvest gig, which was at Goldeneye in Mendocino County.

"It was the best, Darren. You have to work for them. Seriously. Zach, Mikey and Pancho are seriously the best. So cool. I had my own Duckhorn truck, cruising around Philo and Boonville, sampling vineyards. It was plush! Way easier than this."

I'd never had an easy wine harvest gig, and with this sort of workload at hand, I found myself fantasizing about an Anderson Valley experience.

"I can email them for you if you're serious," she added.

"I might be," I said.

I encountered more Visa hang-ups. Now Australia immigration was requesting more information regarding my health insurance. They already charged my card $280 for the visa, and if they didn't grant me it, I'll probably never return here.

At dinner that night, which was mashed potatoes with beef and gravy on it, Kim said out loud at the table, "Darren, let's go swimming and drink Riesling after work." Poor Hjeinte's eyes went sad. It was a tempting offer, but I wasn't about to go there, in spite of the desert of sexuality I was traipsing through.

* * *

Wednesday that week couldn't have gone any worse. Harvest was bottlenecking as Matt Wenk had said it would, and with abundant yields in the vineyards, all the barrels full of 2009 wine had to be forklifted out of Marananga for space and trucked over to the Rocland facility that Two Hands rented out. And from Rocland, all the barrels that Heintje was emptying for bottling were going to be sent back to Marananga for us to wash and prepare for this vintage's wine. Ben said it was something he was pushing for them to do way before harvest, but Michael and Matt hadn't finalized the blends for 2009 in time.

I'm used to moving wine via truck when you pump it out of barrels and into tanks, but not full on barrels double stacked on racks, with straps securing them to the truck in the dusty open air. However, it made sense to me and saved a movement of wine through a pump in the end. That's how they do things here, and since Kim and I were the only two workers at Marananga, she hammered out multiple yeast inoculations inside, while I racked the White Fronti off its lees into a smaller tank and busted out a round of pump overs while stepping out to drive the forklift periodically to unload fruit and load up "Cool Gary's" semi-trailer with 64 full barrels of wine.

The obvious fear while conducting this task was dropping a barrel, and since the Australian preference for barrel is bigger, all the more expensive wine to lose. Plus the side shifter option on the forklift wasn't available, since we'd installed the bin dumper forks that spin loads upside down, so each stack had to be aligned perfectly by the driver. The trailer had enough room for thirty barrels on each side, back to back, so while putting on the last thirty, you had to be cognizant of not pushing the forks into the backs of the barrels that were already stacked.

The only specific instruction for the job from Matt was "no Cabernet or Grenache barrels," but earlier he pointed at the entire center stack of barrels inside and said, "most of these can go too." Everything had to go eventually, so his commands were confusing. Of course I loaded up twelve barrels and realized the code on the barrels was indeed Grenache. I started unloading them, much to Gary's dismay, who had to untie and unlatch the stacks *and* smoke about four more cigarettes for patience. At one point I had Chelsea come out of the lab to double check the codes for me, and she called Ben about it. I was out there in the heat unloading more Grenache barrels from the truck when Ben pulled up in his green Toyota Camry.

"Matt says it's cool: Grenache can go!" he yelled.

"Fuck!" I said, stomping the gas and bringing those barrels back out and onto the truck. As I was nearly done, with way too much time already invested in what should've been a simple endeavor, the forklift ran out of gas with a rack of Grenache barrels slightly raised in the air. I punched the little steering wheel and screamed "Of course! Fuck!" I hopped off and undid the gas cylinder, storming back to the tank behind the winery. As I started filling the portable tank, I realized that the main tank was nearly out of propane too, but I wasn't ready to believe it. I stood there for 20 minutes, hoping my little tank would fill. Cool Gary came back there to check on me.

"Mate, how ya going?" he said with a cigarette smelling whiff.

"Just filling this Gary. It's slow man."

"It's close to six mate."

"I know. Let's give it a try."

I disconnected the hose and rushed the cylinder back to the forklift. It didn't feel any heavier. As I opened the valve and hopped back on, the forklift fired up and I completed the stack. There were only four more barrels to load on and as I hauled ass to get them, the forklift sputtered out of gas again. I leaned my head down and nearly cried. There was still fruit to crush, another round of pump overs to do, let alone following Gary to Rocland and unloading him there, all before the dinner hour of seven. Gary was sitting in a chair by the cellar roll up door and he stood when he saw me take the tank off again to fill. Around the back, I double checked the connection, and opened the master valve. This time it seemed to be filling the tank, but still on the slow side. Ten minutes later Gary came around again.

"Gary I'm sorry man. I think this master tank is empty."

"Let's have a look," he said, checking the gauge. "Naw says there's still some gas, not much though."

I finally got Gary loaded up just after 6 PM. I ran inside to use the bathroom and brew a shot of espresso within a two minute time frame. By the time I pulled out of the Marananga parking lot to follow Gary over to Rocland, I'd lost him. Without a phone, which every other intern had invested in but me, I had to go instinctual on where this facility was that I'd only been to twice before. I remembered the outlying highway where you could see Rocland, but couldn't get there. After 20 minutes of failed attempts, I pulled into Nuriootpa, starving, and called Ben on a payphone.

"Where the hell is Rocland?" I said.

He laughed. "Ah man. You're not there yet?

"No. I lost Cool Gary. Not one of my finest moments over here."

He gave me instructions, but followed them with "no one will be there. They close up at five."

"Really?"

"Yeah mate."

"There's like sixty plus barrels on the truck that need to get loaded in," I said.

"Yeah, no one's there."

"Can you call Hjeintje to come back there to unload?"

"I'll call Matt," Ben said.

I actually felt like quitting then and there. Not that it was the job, but it was me. Here I was, thinking I had what it takes to be a winemaker at a prestigious winery, and again I was completely unprepared and lame. I clenched the wheel and realized that it would be a favor to Two Hands to throw in the towel and get out of their way. With apprehension and this realization in mind, I got to Rocland to face the music and Gary's skin cancerous glare, but instead saw the miracle of a parked motorcycle and a generous, much gossiped about Barossan unloading the semi on a forklift. Tears welled in my eyes.

"Heintje! Thank you," I said with a disturbing enthusiasm, like I'd been saved out at sea.

"For what, this?" he said, then nervously snorted.

"Yes. You need a hand?"

"No mate, go grab dinner."

Back in the truck with the sun gleaming white and pink over the dusty Barossa and its yellowing leaves of its vineyards, I repaired myself mentally and let most of the weight go. I still felt like a wildcard employee as I pulled up to the entire Two Hands staff seated outside of Marananga at a table drinking wine and having dinner. I parked, feeling like everyone there had heard of my moronic endeavors, but no one knew. Everyone had been busy with their own escapades.

"Darren! I saved you a glass of this," Kim announced as I sat down sheepishly at the end of the table next to Matt, handing me the last of a bottle of white wine from Western Australia. I could've drunk a 24 ounce pour of that in a second. She was seated at the opposite end of the long table, with Calie at the head, Timmy across from her, and Michael Rizzo and Chelsea down the line. Matt and Ben were next to each other, with Gareth and Nathan in the mix. Michael Twelftree wasn't there for this feast.

"How ya going?" Matt said with a sparkle in his eye and smirk, then jabbed me in the side, knowing I'd had a shitty day.

"Not my finest, but it's all there now," I admitted.

"So Matt," Calie suddenly spoke up, his tan face smiling. Calie was a friendly, young, strong guy from what I knew of him, and was apparently getting stuck with a streak of the torridly long night shifts. The heads around him suspiciously went to their plates. I took the whole glass of whatever it was down the hatch in a single swig. "We need to talk to you about these hours. This schedule."

Matt had a big bite of food in his mouth. "These hours?" he said through the food. "Whaddya mean Calie?"

"Well in the contract it says we won't work more than twelve hour shifts, and have a day off every week."

"Yeah," Timmy leaned in, adding to Calie's confrontation.

"It's vintage mate," Matt said.

"We are doing like fourteen, fifteen hour shifts, and I have not had a day off in ten days," Calie pointed out.

"When's your day off, Calie?" Matt asked.

"Sunday."

"That's in three days. You can get through it, right mate?"

"It's the night shift that is getting the bad part." That was true. In spite of the day's frustration, the morning shift was the best shift, since you started at seven, and finished by seven, with a drink filled staff dinner to close out the night. However, night shift started after dinner, and though on paper was supposed to be fewer hours and more easygoing, the bulk of wine grapes were being delivered in the afternoon and evening, leaving the night workers busy until nine in the morning.

"What's going on at night, Nathan?" Matt asked his cellar hand.

"There's just so much, Matt. It's full on."

Calie leaned forward to continue. "The work is okay, but we need more pay."

"More pay? You're asking for more money now?" Matt threw his fork down.

"We're doing fifteen hours on night shift," Timmy added. "So I think more money to make up for that is what Calie is saying."

"It just makes sense," Michael Rizzo added.

"As you eat your dinner that we hired a chef for, every night, with good booze, you all are going to sit there and ask this?"

"It's not just Calie," Gareth clarified, joining the protest.

"We talked about this," Timmy said.

Matt was getting angry. Then he looked over right at me and with wild eyes said, "You too Daz?! You're in on this?"

"This is the first I've heard of this," I said honestly. "I'm okay."

"Matt," Calie continued, "just more pay because this is more than the contract said–"

"Fuck! All right you want more pay? Dinners are done. No more dinners! We'll take the money from that for your 'more pay.'"

Timmy audibly gulped with that threat.

"You all don't know what it takes. This is vintage! Fuck you! Dinner is over. Get back to work!" Matt got up with his plate and stormed off, leaving the rest of us at the table in shocked silence. Calie was blushing red. Nathan was looking at Ben with a crazy face.

"You shouldn't have asked for more money, mate," Ben told Calie.

"It wasn't just Calie," Gareth said. "We all talked about it, and Calie said he'd ask for us."

"Thanks for asking my opinion on it," I said sarcastically. "Would have been nice to know you were going to bring something like that up in advance. Now it's going to be really comfortable around here."

"Yeah you guys are fucked," Nathan said. "I've never seen Matt like that. Hwah!"

We cleaned up our plates and the Branson crew drove off solemnly in a couple Two Hands trucks. Kim and I had another hour of work that we could've left to the night crew, but with the mutiny of the night, we decided to knock it out. There were three tanks that needed to be inoculated, and since my experience mostly entailed working at wineries that didn't do this, I needed Kim and Matt to give me another demo. Everyone was scared to see or talk to Matt after the dinner, even me, but since we were the same age, I figured I'd be the first. It took an hour total to get the yeast to a foamy active level at a cool enough temperature to match the tank's juice temperature to pitch it into. Matt softened up about an hour in, and he and I started talking about surfing and weed. He asked me what parts of Oz I wanted to see while I was here, and I mentioned the Clare Valley.

"Ah the Clare! I'm goin' there Friday. Wanna go?"

Friday was my day off, and in light of the blow up and everything, I couldn't imagine saying no.

"I'm in. For sure."

"Ah cool, you'll meet Bunny." He giggled. I'd seen the word "Bunny" written on a dozen or so barrels, and heard Matt and Twelftree bring the man up in conversation, but had yet to meet him.

CHAPTER 19

Thursday at Marananga, as I checked on the basket press full of Bunny's Block Clare Valley Shiraz and pumped the wine in the pan to tank, Tom Shobbrook pulled up to get four of the orange one ton grape bins for the pick that night. I remembered him from our vineyard tour of the Barossa. This being a small town, I learned that it was his wife that had arranged to grind my bag of coffee beans that I'd flown over from the US at the start of my trip, by way of Blond Coffee in Angaston. I asked him how his family's vineyard was looking and he told me that he'd been converting it to biodynamic farming.

"I make some wine too. You should come out and taste sometime." Out of the corner of my eye I noticed a half dozen orange bins sitting in the sun of already crushed McMurtrie Vineyard Shiraz that needed to be dumped into the tank we had just shoveled out into the press. They were roasting in the sun, and I knew if Matt turned up he'd snap for sure.

"Tom let me get these inside, then I'll load you up," I said.

"Right. Too easy," Tom said.

As I got the last bin into the cool cellar, I drove out and started loading up Tom's truck. When I was finished, Tom asked for my number.

"I didn't get a phone yet," I said.

"Here's mine then," he said, scribbling his number on a piece of paper. "You around tomorrow afternoon? After picking?"

"Yeah, tomorrow could work," he said.

Matt pulled up then and saw me getting his info. He looked amused that I was making a new friend who looked like a Deadhead.

"Ah, Dazza, I see you're gonna hang out with this ruffian?" he joked.

"Yeah," Tom said. "We have matching beards after all."

Once Tom was loaded, I cleaned out the emptied tank and began the process of tipping in each bin of crushed McLaren Vale Shiraz to fill the space. Apparently McMurtrie was the source of some of the finest Shiraz in the cellar here.

It was Ben's birthday, and the crew was still a bit unnerved after last night's plea for pay. Eleni cooked beef schnitzel, which was just the kind of comfort food required for this sort of work, and Matt cracked two really expensive red wines from his own collection to ease the tension. He even served them blind after Timmy's request. We all obviously needed the job, and Two Hands definitely needed us to get through harvest, so the demand for more money pretty much fizzled out immediately, and now we all just wanted to make Matt happy again. There were rumors about the 2009 vintage crew that worked here that had experienced the same abundance of hours, no days off, and no overtime or harvest bonus to compensate it. Some of those people apparently walked off the job, the final blow being premature layoffs and the scheduling of the harvest party an hour away in Adelaide on a night that four of the interns were scheduled to press wine and barrel down at Branson. Ben and Nathan told us the interns got drunk on a tank of Matt's Smidge wine and went on a destructive rampage, leaving a massive load of grapes in the hopper uncrushed, breaking whatever they could, and even heating up hardware like a hammer with the pressure washer and putting the smoldering thing into a barrel of good Grenache. I'm sure bodily fluids topped up barrels too. Knowing that this happened so recently, and that the 2009 team reacted accordingly, had us all fearing for early layoffs and finding ourselves out of money before our return ticket home date, so everyone decided to be quiet and try to restore the peace.

Calie, Kim and I caught a ride home with Ben and had a quick beer at their rental. Ben kept bringing up how Tom Shobbrook had offered me to go to his place and taste. "You'll probably smoke cones and talk about clones," he said, laughing.

"Are his wines good?" I asked.

"The Tommy Ruff sucks balls. But his other wines are good. He does skin contact Riesling, Nebbiolo, Shiraz. He's a soap dodger."

"A what?"

"A hippie, like you."

Ben had never hung out with Tom, didn't even say anything to him when he was showing us his vineyard that day, and was acting like it was weird that I was trying to make a friend. We'd been working in a bubble, and I was ready to branch out a little from the Two Hands tree trunk and see what else was happening in the valley. Since I had the next day off, I couldn't think of a better time to get to know Tommy Ruff and try some small batch creations.

CHAPTER 20

The next morning around six, Timmy sputtered in from night shift, making less of a 12-hour shift of it somehow. The average shift was fourteen hours as of late, and in our sleep deprived, exhausted brains, keeping tabs on people working any less than that was becoming juicy, juvenile detective work. I made coffee and was happy to spend the daylight hours without my certified cellar boots on. Matt pulled up to the train car in his Subaru to get me. I brought a joint in case Matt was keen, but it was a busy day for him in spite of this vineyard check. I was transitioning to night crew, so my day off was technically 24 hours off, but it seemed generous enough. We drove north to the highway and started heading out of town into the low, straw colored hills. Matt was in a good mood and provided some commentary on the Clare, from the ageability of Rieslings ("They get a petrol aroma and more honeyed with age"), to what happens when you break down way out in the middle of nowhere.

"If you ever get lost in Australia, look for the grain silos and you'll find someone," he said.

He told me a story about a mate of his whose car broke down outside of Alice Springs. Couple hours later an elderly couple pulled up and he flagged them down, told them what happened, and the old woman kept saying, "That's terrible," and gave him some food through the cracked window, then rolled it up and they took off. He started yelling and chasing their car, waving his arms and the car drove faster in the distance. Two whole days later, a second car appeared. Matt said he'd heard about people breaking down in the middle of Australia and just climbing up and cutting power lines to get attention. "But then of course you've got to be careful not to electrocute yourself."

The undulating hills of Clare Valley rose out of the flatlands about an hour and a half later. He asked me about my own life, and I talked to him about being divorced, my parents' restaurants on the central coast and how they'd split up too, surfing, and places I've worked.

"Maybe you'll marry someone here, mate," he said, then slapped me on the leg and laughed.

"I'm not opposed to it. Haven't seen any women in the Barossa, so that's one problem."

"Nah, you'll have to go down to Adelaide."

He was married with two kids and lived in Adelaide. He talked about the ups and downs of Australia's wine industry, the high scores that wine critics gave the big, syrupy styles of red wines back in the day, and how most of the high end wine produced here is now exported mainly to Asia and not America. Eventually, down home, shaggy vineyards started appearing just south of Auburn. Matt told me there were seven sub-districts of Clare Valley, with Polish River Hill having all slate for soil.

"So is there a lot of Riesling planted here because of German settlers?" I asked.

"Nah, I think the only white varieties to plant in Australia were Chardonnay, Rizza, and Semillon. Riesling did the best." I asked him about elevation and he said most of Clare was about 400 to 600 meters, which made it cooler than Barossa. He pointed out Mount Horrocks winery and mentioned how the owner married Jeremy Grosset, the Riesling master of the namesake winery. We came into the single-level town center, and it looked larger than Tanunda, with pubs, restaurants, bakeries and some department stores, even a random Sears. It was dated for sure. Matt emergency parked outside of a bakery and ran inside, returning with a couple flaky, savory pies before heading to the Bunny Peglidis vineyard in Watervale to see how the rest of his Shiraz was coming. We pulled up and parked on a sloping property and hit the hard, red dirt. I heard the crackle of talk radio, echoing through the vines. Matt giggled.

"Bunny doesn't like to net for birds, and he doesn't like guns, so he plays the radio during harvest and he thinks it keeps the birds out." He laughed again. There must have been five or more speakers out there.

"Do his neighbors get pissed?" I asked, looking down at the lower neighboring properties and little houses.

"Nah, I don't know. I think they know it's just Bunny."

The black clusters had plenty of flavor, with brown seeds and a nice brightness to the taste. Though Clare is referred to as a cool climate area of South Australia, it still gets hot as Barossa. Apparently there was limestone beneath the terra rossa surface, which gave the wines some mid palate magic. The slopes and undulating hills added some yield reducing terrain, concentrating clusters of Riesling, Shiraz and Cabernet mostly. What I was seeing made the Barossa seem like a flat valley floor in comparison.

"It's about ready," Matt said, spitting out some seeds and looking at me.

Bunny's wife came out to say hello, and Matt introduced me as simply "an American." Bunny had gone into town so we'd miss him, she said, asking me what I thought of Australia so far.

"Love it," I affirmed.

On the drive back Matt pulled off to show me the "Contours" vineyard, and there were senior citizens out there handpicking the terraces in midday heat, with a radio playing classical music. It was surreal to see older white people picking grapes—something you'd never see back home. The men were wearing slacks and tucked in shirts, with berets and hats on, while the ladies were actually in long dresses. It could have been a hundred years ago.

"Is this how all hand picked sites work here?" I asked Matt.

"Yeah, occasionally you'll get some backpackers to pick, or some Vietnamese. But it's mainly geezers."

"It must take forever," I said, seeing them break to hear one guy finish an animated story, drinking coffee, newspapers at arm's reach with chairs to lounge in too. They were talking more than clipping.

Matt got a call from Ben at Branson then, and he affirmed that he'd be there shortly. My day in the Clare was coming to an abbreviated end. Once back into Barossa, Matt dropped me back off at the train car where a slumbering Timmy woke as I entered. "How was it?" he asked.

"It's pretty cool up there. He had to get back early so we didn't taste anywhere." I was due to join nightshift, leaving me about eight hours of free time to burn. I negotiated the use of Timmy's Magna for some offsite activities. The offer of ten bucks for gas sealed the deal. I called Tom Shobbrook and made arrangements to come over later in the afternoon to taste, then I drove to Blond Coffee in Angaston. A car worked wonders for a person's freedom. You don't notice till you go without for awhile.

I headed out to Torbreck to taste. The small stone cellar door not too far from the Marananga winery was ancient and well preserved. I went through all the wines including the flagship Run Rig with Lee Ann, a host not far from my age who was full of knowledge and cracking jokes. We somehow joked about plastic surgery—she had none she clarified—and she said how she and her coworkers say, "That's not original rootstock" when customers come in with Botox or boob jobs. I bought a rosé of Mataro and a bottle of The Steading. I smoked what was left of a joint on Neldner Road and once on Jenke Road I turned in one lot too early up to a single story ranch house with a great view and an outdoor swimming pool. I parked and approached the house, hearing cartoons and some kids inside the house through the screen door. I knocked and said "hello?" This could've been the place, but then I realized what I was looking like, and that my fedora hat, shades and beard alone would've resulted in a very warranted phone call to the Barossa Valley police. I coasted out of there and found Lot 2 Jenke Road and pulled past another house and saw the work sheds in back. This was more like it. Tom came out with his John Lennon shades on, t-shirt, jeans and Birkenstock sandals. I swear he was as stoned as I was, and we chatted while leaning on the rim of a headless double-sized oak barrel that he was soaking up with water to eventually get ready for fermenting in.

"Do you use proxy or anything to clean them?" I asked.

"Nah mate. Fill them with water and let the sun do its UV thing. Have never had a problem."

Inside, the shed was a winemaking zone that was completely operable by one person. Making high quality wine on a small enough scale that industrial machinery and other people weren't necessary was becoming my dream. In America, legal compliance to produce alcohol was expensive. In California, getting a shed like Tom's bonded for wine production was nearly impossible and expensive enough where making only a small amount would put you out of business. He was doing only 12 tons this vintage, as opposed to Two Hands' projected thousand. His wines from last season were aging in barrels stacked three high with wood chalks instead of barrel racks holding them in place. Everything could be done by himself by gravity, even bottling. He mentioned how he made a barrel of Merlot for his mom because she likes it, and a barrel of Shiraz for his dad. His protocol was to use only wild yeasts, no added yeast food, but he did add tartaric acid for balance, reluctantly. "You have to here, mate. The PH's are so high!" His white macro bins full of new fermentations were laid out in the center of the cellar, clean on the inside rims, and sorted with no visible green stems. He had a destemmed bin of skin contact Adelaide Hills "Savage Blanc" as he called it that was just starting to ferment. He's done Shiraz with 20 percent Riesling cofermented in it before. There was a very modest, elegant style to the wines from 2009 that we started tasting, with the main action being the mid-palate and finish.

"You don't have to spit, mate," he pointed out, "it's your day off."

The Shobbrook wines were made in such small production that you had to drink them, or pour what you didn't taste from your glass back in the barrels to do them justice. The wines were shy on the nose, except for a baby-sized barrel Shiraz experiment, which was full of sweet woody notes and blackberry flavors. An old local from the area popped in to say hi and started tasting along with us. He was an old-school Barossa guy who immediately started harassing me for having a day off during vintage. The last wine Tom pulled a sample of was the one Ben told me about, and it was easily the standout: 2009 Adelaide Hills Nebbiolo. He served it in a massive Pinot Noir goblet. Brick-like color, huge rose and tar aromatics and that spicy acidic finish that lingered and made you yearn for a charcuterie platter. When released, it would be $55 a bottle. The old fella left and I asked if I could buy some bottles. "I'll give ya one," he said. I asked for the Shiraz and he flowed me a bottle with "Seppeltsfield District" on the label. His wines weren't distributed in the US, but his wife had been urging him to get his wines into New York City because she used to live there.

"I've got more work to do but if you want to sit outside and have a beer and chat, feel free. It's your day off, after all."

Outside in the sun, he handed me a Coopers and I sat on some pallets as he kept soaking up his other headless barrels. He put on some electronica and I felt it was appropriate to grab the same joint I'd brought up to Clare earlier with Matt that remained unlit. I got it out of the car, kept it in my hand, and kept it there for 30 more minutes trying to find the right moment to break it out. I felt like I was in high school again, wondering if a new friend smoked pot or not. As I finished my beer, he started loading a full barrel of Nebbiolo rosé on a truck to take down to the Adelaide Hills to bottle up for a winery he contracts with. I kept the door to his cellar closed while he pallet jacked some barrels out of the way. He stopped and took a bung out of a barrel and smelled the wine inside.

"Huh," he said.

"What's that?" I asked.

"A Grenache I made that I don't like. Now it smells good."

"It changed, in a good way?"

"Grenache is so weird man," he said. "I almost dumped this a couple months ago."

Back outside I decided to just give him the joint and get out of his working way. "Well Tom I'm gonna jam and get my roommate's car back to him. Thanks a lot for everything."

"Ah no worries."

"I wanted to give you this," I said with an outstretched palm holding the sweaty mangled looking thing.

"Oh no. No thanks man. I don't smoke actually."

"Oh really?" I laughed.

"Yeah, I mean, I used to be really into it, but it started making me forget stupid things all the time. Now I just focus on my booze."

"So you reached a point where you just felt you had to stop?"

"Yeah. I love growing it. It's such a beautiful plant. SA is a perfect place for it. There's heaps of it around and quite cheap."

"Yeah. Well, shoot, well uh, thanks again. Maybe we can hang out again when things wind down?"

"Yeah we'll do dinner. I'll stop by the winery and get a hold of you."

I sputtered off, thinking about generalizations and hoping Tom Shobbrook wasn't disappointed in the one I'd made. His winery had inspired me and his comment about forgetting stupid things all the time lingered with me for the rest of the afternoon. We were the same age, but he was a good five years ahead of me at least.

CHAPTER 21

I entered a vicious night shift schedule that night, making that day off where I impersonated an American wine tourist a very distant, unobtainable memory. I started hallucinating around 5 AM on one of the mornings as I completed the Marananga pump overs for Gareth, seeing shapes in the light, fellow casuals when they weren't there down on the winery floor, and fermentation bubbles turning into eyeballs. When you have 30 tanks to pump over on your own, your mind travels to distant territories.

We had a staff dinner one of the nights at Greenock Pub. Timmy requested a to go box and asked everyone with food left on their plates if he could take it all home.

"That's gross," Nathan said, offended even as Timmy scooped in part of his chicken schnitzel.

"I'm still in college mode," Timmy said with a smile.

"Ha!" Calie exclaimed, smiling at me. "A scraper!" Though he pronounced it slightly wrong, I tried to distinguish a "scrapper" from a "scraper" right there at the table with Calie, but came out with them meaning pretty much the same thing. Timmy just laughed and kept collecting food scraps into his box.

Both winery facilities were loaded down with Shiraz. I spent ten hours straight just doing pump overs and cool downs. Everything was actively fermenting at both Marananga and Branson and needed care. I got home after sunrise, had a couple slabs of bread with cheese and prosciutto, a glass of Max's Garden Shiraz, and then got into bed. It was stormy outside, and chilly enough to use the choo-choo's questionable heater. I thought they'd find me and the entire derailment reduced to ashes in no time the way it rattled and roared. I dreamt of a street corner like the one my bank was on back in California. I was walking, waiting to cross the street at the intersection, and I noticed brown snakes beneath the florist stand on the corner, and then more underneath a little visible cavern. I alerted the florist in the dream and she didn't believe me. Then I saw a huge one slink out and start chasing a toddler. A baby brown snake hissed out in my direction and I started running for my life.

* * *

On my eighth straight evening of nightshift duty, I began smoking weed on break. It was warfare now. Branson. I became one of the Bransonites. The mortal warriors, often covered in yeast and filth. Marananga was like Beverly Hills in comparison. My hands were losing feeling, and the slit on my finger may have been fostering multiple strains of brettanomycees. The night before was a messy one. A big potter tank that was being emptied via gravity into the press below had sheathed a massive juice pocket that absolutely blew out like a purple mortar blast and coated the place and our crew with sludge. We had thought all the juice had drained out and it was time to open the little door to allow the skins to fall, but were dead wrong. I had Chelsea take a photo of the aftermath, which Nathan didn't appreciate too much since he was the manager on duty. He got annoyed with me to some extent, but liked my jokes enough. I asked Ben at some point if Nathan was at Two Hands for the wine or the job, and he said the job.

Later in the evening shift, Nathan asked me to do the task of holding the must hose over the drain in the cellar while he pushed with hot water from out at the crusher. Once grapes started coming down the line, he said he'd run in and help me get the line up the mobile stepladder and over the top of the tank, also referred to as "getting it up." There was so much weight in the hose at that point that it was an impossible solo feat, and it entailed tying the hose to the top of the tank so the crushed grapes could pump their way up and down into the tank. There were two 5-ton capacity fermenter tanks we were using for 9 tons of freshly delivered Clare Valley Shiraz, so we'd have to stop in between filling both to do the same up and down thing. I was holding the line, letting the water pour straight into the floor drain at the base of the mobile stairs, and there was just water, water, and water. I heard Chelsea and Nate's distant voices talking over full on crushing mode. Then I saw the dark grape line approaching in the massive hose. Surely Nathan remembered and was going to stop the crusher to help me get the line up now. I tried to start walking the hose up the stairs myself but it was too heavy, wet and dangerous. The crushed fruit started blasting out the end like a firehose filled with a purple smoothie. "Stop!" I screamed from inside the enclosed cellar. Nothing. "Stop!" I shouted again. Grapes and juice were splattering out while I held the hose upright in the air. I didn't know what do. "Stop!" I yelled again, this time dropping the hose and running outside to yell a fourth time. I heard Nate finally tell Chelsea to turn the crusher off, realizing what happened. He ran in to see almost a quarter of a ton on the ground and me covered in juice.

"Are ya all right mate?" he sheepishly asked.

He didn't apologize, but he picked up a squeegee and swept some of the mess into a pile, then helped me get the hose up top. We filled both tanks with crushed fruit to full capacity, and as we were pushing with water to clear the lines later on, he came in and said, "The rest of the evening should be cruisy." I pumped over the new tank, got a sample bottle for the lab, then we hauled over to Marananga to sit on the back of the 3.5 ton capacity forklift as it loaded 5.3 tons of skins into the press. I took a break and microwaved some of the beef and rice leftovers and almost puked with one sip of the pitch black 2008 Ares that Gareth was in there racking from tank into brand new hogshead barrels for the final six months of its aging process. "Two hundred percent new oak!" he exclaimed. I had a coffee which made the acid reflux worse. So little I've learned about myself in all of these years.

Around five in the morning, Nathan and I went back to Branson on the dirt back roads and we braked hard for the first kangaroo I'd seen in this country. "Hwah!" he said as he swerved a little and came to a halt. It was a haggard skinny looking one, not all too different from a Paso Robles deer.

"That's the first one I've seen," I said.

"Hwah, really?"

"Yeah."

In that late night delirium, the ginger cellar hand smiled, perhaps a little proud of this Australian mascot, and we drove on to clean up Branson and shut things down until the morning crew arrived.

The morning light came upon us. Matt showed up in board shorts, a blue work shirt and fluorescent green flip flops, chapped that the Clare grower sent almost two tons extra that night. Because of the extra amounts, the two tanks we'd crushed into would surely spill out the top during the rise of fermentation. It was 7:10 AM, ten minutes past quitting time. I thought we were done, but we had to head back to the other facility to help their night crew finish up. There had been some hold ups there with the press, and Gareth, Kim and Chelsea were delirious trying to get things done. The morning crew was having coffee and getting ready to start doing simple pump overs since there wasn't any fruit to crush yet. I turned into a pretty self-centered prick and toyed with saying "you guys suck" when 7:30 rolled around and they hadn't started working, but I didn't. Then I broke my black frame prescription glasses while washing a tank and had to duct tape them back up. I was wet and cold, and the juice stained sleeves of my hoodie were 15 degrees *Baume* and kicking into fermentation. I snuck a siphon of Ares Shiraz lees into two empty milk cartons that fit perfectly into my backpack for a later, creamier consumption.

Nathan dropped me off at the choo-choo around eight and I got in bed with a glass of Ares and passed out only one sip in. When I woke up at 2 PM the bed looked like an abortion was conducted on the sheets.

CHAPTER 22

I got an email from Fiona at Barossa Collective to see if I could play a gig at 6:30 PM on Friday March 19th. Timmy and I met her before harvest started when we stopped in to her tasting room and event space and tried a handful of wines. I immediately agreed to play and got an okay from Matt to leave an hour early for it. The morning of the gig when I got to Branson with Nathan, we discovered that all the Bransonites were gone and had left without hot washing bins and cleaning the crusher area like Matt had asked them too. Nathan was disappointed but got down to business as usual. Heintje was allegedly in charge, and his current flame was working over at Marananga, which he could surely sniff from across Seppeltsfield, ultimately drawing him away from his post and leaving us to sort it out.

I started upstairs pump overs anyway, and heard Nate ring up Matt and start spewing, "Matt, there's nobody at Branson." I heard him saying it again in regards to the night crew's absence. Matt misunderstood that to mean even I hadn't shown up. Matt arrived at Marananga and apparently went off on them for being there, ordering Timmy to drive to the train cars to pick me up, and sending Heintje back to Branson to wash bins and clean the crusher for the day's fruit intake. I saw Timmy's red car pull up first about 8:15 AM and I waved down to him while switching over a pump over.

"Darren! Does Nathan know you're here?" he asked.

"Yeah!"

"Then why did he tell Matt you weren't? Is Trent here too?"

"Yeah man." I ran down a flight to disconnect the lower hose from the valve and move it to the next tank in line. Every tank had to be done so this would be my entire morning's work.

Timmy stormed up to Nate and demanded to know why he told Matt he was all alone. The kid was right up in his face. "Get fucked, Timmy,"

Nathan replied. Heintje arrived and started bringing up empty barrels for filling, flooring it angrily on the forklift. I saw Matt pull up in his Subaru and park. Timmy went over to talk to him, then he walked back to the base of the towers.

"Hey Darren! Matt wants me to take you to Marananga to help Chelsea."

I stopped the pump over and charged over, grabbing my bag with my hat, harmonicas and change of clothes for the night's gig. We drove over to Marananga, going over the mass-miscommunication. Timmy was working 7 PM to 7 AM, so I asked him if he could come to work at 6 PM (we had a special staff tasting of all the 2008 wines scheduled) and let me use his car to get to the gig.

"Yeah, I'm running pretty much on empty," he said as we passed Seppeltsfield winery's palm tree row.

"I'll put some gas in."

We got to Marananga and as he idled, I ran in and got my guitar, quickly packing it in the trunk, since I'd be using his car to get there. I thanked him again and got to work.

Cut to 6:20 PM at Two Hands Marananga and still no Timmy. I was at the lab desk and the winery phone rang.

"Good evening, Two Hands winery," I said.

"Um hey," a little chuckle on the line. "It's Timmy. I'm out of gas."

"You're out of gas?"

"Yeah we're broken down at the roundabout."

"No!"

"Can you have someone get us and bring some gas?" he asked.

"Man, I'm late for my show."

"Yeah. Can you ask Matt?"

"All right. I'll see what Matt wants to do."

I hung up, said "goddamnit," and my mind started to percolate.

I walked outside on the crush pad where Matt was manning the press and talking to a Lallemand yeast rep. I told him what happened, how Timmy was waiting for my gas money and didn't fill up, and how I was going to be late for the show I was supposed to play.

"Tightass Timmy! What, are you going to put two dollars in?" he exclaimed. "Fuck, take a Ute to the gig. Don't worry about it mate."

I jumped in the truck and sped toward the Barossa Valley highway, 6:23 on the dash with the show starting at 6:30. Then I realized "Fuck my guitar is in Timmy's trunk!" Got to the roundabout and didn't see them. Drove into Tanunda searching the other intersections and no luck. 6:30 now. Drove to Kim and Calie's, backtracked toward Marananga and Tanunda and up to Nuri: no red Magna on the side of the road. I wanted to kill him by this point. I was driving and screaming, and had come to the conclusion that he would be clobbered on sight. I looked around the Ute cab for possible objects for violence. A rope was in there. I sped back to the winery. Not having a cell phone was my main fault in this, if not trusting Timmy. I pulled into the lot at the winery and saw Matt on the forklift out there and Timmy's red Magna among the employee cars. I parked, got out, and Matt paused on the forklift.

"What happened?" he asked. "Did they boo you off stage already?"

I opened Timmy's trunk and pulled out my guitar and held it up.

"Ah!" Matt exclaimed with his arms up.

"I'm gonna fucking kill him!" I said. I chucked the guitar in the passenger side of the Ute when I heard footsteps cautiously approaching.

"I tried to flag you down," Timmy said. I turned around, my beard practically in Satanic flames no doubt, while he and Heintje came toward me with wine glasses in hand.

"Spend some fucking money, Timmy! You fucking asshole! Do you realize what the fuck you just did?!" I slammed my harmonica holder in the door. Heintje's hands went in his pockets and Timmy threw his arms up helplessly and turned around and hurried back inside the winery. I floored it out of the lot and up into Angaston, arriving in a manic state at 7:05 to a forgiving tranquil glass of Radford Riesling and the good company of fellow employees Gareth and Michael Rizzo, and Fiona, who was more worried about my safety than my tardiness. I was picturing 25 people paying 40 bucks each for this dinner and sitting around in silence for the first 30 minutes. She had some flamenco sounds playing on a speaker outside. The first course had yet to be served. I sat in the chair with Ben's guitar and my harmonica and started an instrumental set.

Gareth and Michael got going a couple hours later. Fiona asked me to stay and drink more, which led me to believe something was happening here. Her knowledge of wine was impressive, and her passion for the Eden Valley had made me a believer in the high elevation region. It was refreshing to get to know a new person, to flirt some, and mainly not to be working for a change. She closed up shop and we went across the street to the Angaston pub where everyone knew her. She ordered a couple beers and handed me a cold Coopers, talking to some guys at the bar. Two drunks at the pool table soon started harassing me, asking me if I was Jewish. I told them I wasn't, but they kept inquiring to the point where I thought things were going to get nasty. One of the guys, wearing a sleeveless shirt and with spiky hair, was inches from my face, analyzing my features and staring me down. Finally he backed away and said, "I guess you must just be a Skippy Poof!"

"What's a skippy poof?" I asked, not really wanting to know but glad that things were getting less neo-Nazi.

He started laughing, hammered, and then got word from the bartender that his mom was there to pick him up and drive him home.

Fiona and I played a game of pool, drank another round of beers, and we started getting a bit touchy along the way. Guys in the bar kept blatantly staring at us as we laughed and I flailed on the cue. I was complimenting her wine shop and her appearance, and in turn she said my guitar playing had been lovely and wanted me to play every Friday night. She kept texting somebody on her phone. When we finished our game she took my hand and said, "let's go drink more wine in the shop!"

We walked back to the tasting room and, to my surprise, a tall, built guy was waiting for her out front. "Hey darl'," she said to the guy, embracing him as I cautiously awaited my introduction. He started groping her and kissing her on the mouth, briefly breaking to shake my hand. She unlocked the door and we headed inside to the tasting bar area. My midnight antics would be reduced to wine, so I drank more from opened bottles. Even though she deflected his hands now and then, he kept pulling her in for make out sessions right in front of me. I was drunk at this point so I used the bathroom, then tried to sleep on the floor in the back inventory room as they started really going at it. I heard gasping and moaning eventually. Fiona woke me a bit later and got me out of there so she could drive home, so I slept in the Two Hands Ute for three hours with a stick shift up my ass, and drove to Branson by 7, still drunk and dressed in my troubadour gear. Matt found it amusing.

"Hwah. You look like shit, Daz," Nathan added.

That day, Ben was in charge of both facilities and frowning from the start. There were no coffee breaks and he kept barking at the team to get things done, and making fun of anyone who was lagging or making mistakes. I was getting on with him okay, managing to make him laugh a few times and, of course, filling him in on my odd nocturnal escapade with Fiona. He was sure to let me know that a skippy poof is a gay kangaroo, and was thrilled that I was called that by an Angaston bogan. Since it was Ben's first vintage to really shine as the assistant, he was under pressure. When I showed up to give Chelsea a dozen more tank samples, she sighed and told me she was sick of him, as he was calling her every half hour for lab results on freshly crushed fruit so we could make the appropriate adjustments before fermentation, and telling her she sucked. He was kind of joking with that part of it, telling me I sucked too, but the overworked team wasn't in the mood for any derogatory humor at this stage of the harvest. She mostly had the luxury of working in the lab at Marananga, with internet access, espresso, leftovers and the like, so I didn't feel too sorry for her.

I had a hard run on the forklift with the task of organizing everything that was already in barrel and stacking them as high as possible for extra, usable space. I finally resigned from the lift at 6:45 pm after my five-high barrel stack kept arching perilously to the left. We needed all the vertical space we could get at both facilities for barrels, as the vintage was turning out to be more plentiful than 2009. Otherwise, I felt I'd succeeded, making way for up to two more rows of barrels in racks. I was sweaty, hungover, and exhausted, and at least twenty tons of fruit were landing any moment.

* * *

After waking up at 3:30 pm the next day, which was my official single day off in nine days, I headed on foot past Penfolds straight to the Sip n' Save. A young employee inside with a mullet and shaved sides of his head was hustling certain cheap wine brands to me to no avail. I chose a Skillogalee Clare Valley Riesling, which Chef Eleni had recommended.

"This is wild," I said, pointing to the cars backed up in their drive thru area. "Heavy drive thru scene. You can't do that at home."

"Do what?" the guy asked.

"Buy booze in your car."

"You're missing out mate. It's the Aussie way." He held his arms up. "Lazy as fuck!"

I walked further into Nuri to activate my new Australian bankcard and shop for next week's snacks at the bakery and grocery store. I stocked up on pears, cheese and cured meats, and gambled on a package of day old vegemite scrolls at the bakery, which resembled cinnamon rolls but were filled with green paste and cheese. I grabbed an espresso and sat on the patio at the bakery, taking in the sleepy, real life happenings of downtown Nuriootpa on a Sunday afternoon, which weren't much.

Back at the train car and in a Riesling induced haze, I began chatting on Facebook with Laura's friend Ava who I met at the bar at the Wheatsheaf Hotel when I first arrived. I was in dire need of some company, and my current lack of a female companion made me think back on my relationship with Grace and the way I'd ended things with her before this adventure. I hadn't felt any sadness at all about calling it off. Now it would've been nice to chat with her, email her about what I was up to, and look forward to her whimsical replies, let alone an erotic self portrait or two. But I was fully unattached, my inbox mostly empty besides the occasional note from my mom, dad and brother, and with Fiona clearly out of the mix, engaging with this hip, rockabilly Adelaide girl in a simple chat bubble was rocking my world. I had turned into a blue collar working man, more than a sensitive, wine-loving, singer-songwriter type, and it was showing in the way I was thinking about girls. I may have even used the phrase "I need to get laid" for the first time in my life to Ben that week. Ava seemed to appreciate the forward commentary, and said she needed to get me out of the Barossa to show me her city.

As the next round of hardcore work resumed, my only pleasure aside from drinking the epic Burgundy and Chateauneuf-du-Pape wines that Michael Twelftree shared every evening at staff dinner was Facebook chatting with Ava. She was heavily flirty and I was coming off as a blue balled coal miner at best. After seven more days in a row of nothing but work, I arranged to take the Link SA bus on a Monday morning from Tanunda to Central Adelaide, where she was going to meet me. I hadn't left the Barossa in over five weeks.

CHAPTER 23

At long last, Timmy dropped me off for the Adelaide-bound morning bus on his way to work. We were trying to reconnect after our friendly fallout and his near loss of his facial structure on my part. He even sort of offered me the use of his car for my city adventure, but I wasn't about to take advantage of the sort-of-sweet kid. He had this huge smirk going on the drive to town, knowing that I was off to see a flesh and blood woman.

I paid the 18.20 and boarded the bus for the ride south to the city. I was nervous heading down. I had been ultra flirty online with Ava many nights leading up to this, a girl I didn't even know, so my shyness was bound to arise once I arrived in person. I looked out over all the vineyards that had been harvested with leaves yellowing on the vine. We'd been so busy. Everyone up here had. There wasn't a lot of fruit left out there from what I could see out the window.

Once in Adelaide, I started toe tapping and even biting my fingernails as the bus pulled into the station. Ava was there waiting in the garage where the bus ultimately parked. She wore large sunglasses, jeans, and a tight t-shirt and welcomed me with a warm, perfumed hug. "How ya goin'?" she asked me. She was more beautiful than I remembered her, hair black as night, and I couldn't get over how I was suddenly transported into the company of a hot woman. We headed for the central market in her little silver car. "I need a coffee," she said.

We went to the Cibo café by the central market. She knew the barista who was back there handling the morning rush. We got a table on the street side and talked about music and restaurants mostly, a very slight hint of anxiousness, probably more on my part, then she picked up a call and her friend Alex soon joined us. Alex was tan and slender with long blonde hair and showed up with a huge dog and a small one in tow. She ordered a coffee from the barista and returned with an artistically frothed latte, asking me about myself, venting about dog sitting the larger animal, then Ava told me about the Italian immigration history in South Australia that brought their elder generations here after WWII. I felt like an imposter, just sitting on the street with two beautiful girls in the city of Adelaide, talking and laughing street side. Meanwhile my colleagues at Branson were surely soaked in filth. Alex finished her coffee and said it was nice to meet me, hugged Ava and headed off with the canines.

Ava and I went to a barebones Italian eatery inside the central market, which was a large space downtown packed with vendor stalls and open most days of the week. I got the day-drinking started with two glasses of Rockford Alicante Bouschet Rosé to be paired with a gnocchi carbonara. The central market was as good as Ben said it was. Bakers, butchers, the Smelly Cheese Company, organic produce stands, Greek, Italian, Asian, and every kind of food available. I bought some organic Mexican coffee and had it ground for me. By the time we dropped into East End Cellars, I was comfortable and cracking jokes with her. They had stacks of Tom Shobbrook's wines in front of the tasting counter and the new releases from Spinifex. I splurged and picked up a chilled Spinifex "Luxe" rosé, a Spinifex "Esprit" red, and a Yangarra Mourvédre. I was on a little spree that I somehow could afford.

Back at Ava's two-story flat behind the artsy Melbourne Street strip in North Adelaide, I cracked the Luxe and she started pulling up music on her computer to play. Her friend Yanni showed up, a doppelganger for actor Aaron Eckhart. At first I thought the same thing that had happened with Fiona was happening here, but he was simply a good friend checking me out presumably. He was engaging, asking me about the Barossa, raving about how good of a singer Ava was, and sharing the best venues for live music in the city. I tried calling a guy named "Sporno" on Ava's phone for an ounce of weed to no avail. Instead I rolled a spliff with Yanni's tobacco and we got ultra high on her small outdoor patio. Ava didn't smoke and got bored with our silence. We formulated a plan to meet for Thai food at Tiger Lily.

On the way, Ava took me into Melbourne Street Cellars, which was right behind her flat. There was a well curated selection at "Melly Street," which was a dark, wood racked, old school bottle shop that sold cigars and liquor too. I almost sprung for my first Grosset Riesling in the cold case but played it cool with a Crabtree Watervale Riesling at a fraction of the price. I was starting to wonder if there was anything that set those different Clare Valley Rieslings apart from each other, or if they all showed perfect lemon lime flavors, no oak, mouthwatering acidity and quick turnaround time from fermentation to bottle. Ava and I reunited with Yanni for a boozy, spicy meal at Tiger Lily next door with the Riesling, shrimp pad Thai, tofu, and chicken skewers in peanut sauce. As we headed out, Yanni and I hugged and I said I hoped to see him again.

Back to her place at sunset, she selected some soul music, then she got changed and came down her stairwell wearing knee high black boots, a short skirt, low-cut black top and leather jacket around it. She wore bright red lipstick. "You look so hot Ava," I said.

"You should smoke again and then we'll go," she advised. Was she not a total catch? What man gets to be in the presence of a knockout who urges him to take a toke before their date? I hadn't even changed either. I stepped out to blaze the rest of the joint, then we walked down to her tapas bar called "Cosecha" and it was the swankiest, late-evening chill spot ever. All these private, make-out-friendly enclaves, blocked strategically by wicker fencing, illuminated by the glow of dark red lighting and the sounds of Modest Mouse. The red light on the window and lurkiness of the place whispered "Amsterdam." She proudly introduced me to her friendly staff of four back in the narrow kitchen area. Then we grabbed a taxi and went to the University for the Northern Lights show, where projectors painted different lit up color schemes on the front of the ancient buildings on campus. "Thanks for taking me to this," I said to her as we sat on a bench looking at one. I ventured my arm around her waist and she instantly put her hand on my thigh.

"Oh sure," she said.

We walked arm in arm down hill back to Melbourne Street to Cosecha. It was at full capacity then, with Beach House playing on the system. She guided me to a tucked away table and had me sit and wait while she got our wine service going. They specialized in small plates, cheese and charcuterie mostly, with olives, bread and a few other wine friendly snacks. The renegaded Two Hands 2008 Ares Shiraz that I'd poured from milk carton to emptied bottle of Max's Garden that morning provided plenty of additional lust for the evening. As we sat there and her staff shuffled about, I placed an arm around the back of the booth. We were hidden from the other patrons, which was the point of the place, and as we drank the full on Shiraz, she urged me to try one of the desserts. A massive chocolate cake on ice cream with sultry strawberries and whipped cream came out. "I need your help with this," I said.

"Oh, you'll do all right."

I ate most of it, which paired with the 17 percent alcohol Ares better than I'd thought. We chatted some more, and in the midst of one silence I said, "Would your staff care if I started making out with you in here?"

"I don't give a fuck about them."

I leaned in and we started "pashing" hardcore. I probably had lipstick all over my face. We made out till the Ares and the last customers were gone, then we walked out around midnight with the staff as they closed up and strutted back to her place. She clicked on an ambient playlist for music and cracked a Tempranillo-Cab from Spain, where we drank and made out some more on the couch, before retreating upstairs to her bedroom.

In the late morning she was up before me, cleaning downstairs before jumping back into bed. She bounced on me and said "Do you want some coffee or breakfast?"

She made me eggs on toast, then drove me to the bus station by 12:30. I was on night shift that night, starting at 7 PM at staff dinner. My bus was there. We kissed in her car before I pulled away and thanked her for showing me a great time.

"I'll be back again," I said.

"You better be," she said with a smile.

CHAPTER 24

I immediately re-entered harvest hell that evening. Everyone was reaching their boiling point as more and more Grenache and late ripening lots were being delivered by vineyard owners. The hottest conversational point was how many tons we'd already processed, how many more were coming, and how much longer Two Hands was going to keep us working. Matt and Michael kept assuring us that the quality of wines we were making was some of the best in Two Hands history. For those of us passionate about wine, that bit of news was inspiring enough to keep us trudging on through the never-ending work hours, which entailed crushing, pumping over, pressing, *and* filling barrels with the new wine. I was the only one who'd gotten away from the Barossa at all, and that experience had tempered my flames.

Timmy was on the phone with his "investor" in the train car before our shift one of the mornings.

"I need to cancel payment into my mutual fund this month," he said to the New Yorker on the line, who was in charge of funneling the flow to his checking account.

That particular shift was busy, hectic, and chaotic. The accountant from the city office named Ben turned up for his official Two Hands "day in the cellar" that the winery made every year-round employee do during vintage. His hair was gelled up and he wore his expensive blue jeans and a new Two Hands work shirt with a high-visibility vest. Matt was busy dealing with Twelftree and Phil the CFO, so Ben was standing around a bit awkwardly without direction. Gareth was hesitant to give him orders and frankly too busy to devote the time for any training. I dug out a five ton fermenter and Calie drove the full wet basket of skins out of the cellar and loaded it in the press. Ben was standing there observing the contraption as I programmed the press cycle, thinking I was setting it at "5" which is the lightest start, but the steel press plate roared down hard and didn't stop. A normal press cycle was 45 minutes, with the plate squeezing its way down in gentle little stages. Whatever cycle I pressed made it come straight down all in one blast. The press pan was filling fast, so I casually walked past Ben to the pump like I knew what I was doing and turned it on, but an air bubble clogged the line. I swiftly unscrewed the hose, as Ben stood at the press watching the wine fill up. He mumbled something like "oh no" or "it's coming" and gyrated a little. I thought nothing too out of the ordinary was going on, then I heard a god-like farting noise as clumps of skins shot out of the top and sides of the press while wine splashed out of the pan. Ben took splatters all over his jeans and vest and abandoned ship. I stopped the cycle and hosed the evidence down and gave it another try. Calie was out there now, wondering what was going on. I hit the same setting and the press plate came swiftly down, breaking wind with grape skins like bullets, actually hitting the HR manager Amanda's window two stories high. Gareth ran out and took an eyeful of skins and shouted, "What the fuck?!" All I was thinking was how lucky I was that Matt Wenk wasn't in range to see this.

I retracted the press plate and stepped away. "I don't think I'm cut out to operate this thing, Gareth," I said. "Setting it at five, right?"

He rinsed his face off and came over, showing me how to actually choose the right setting, which was definitely not the fifth one. He gave me a stern look as the press plate came down appropriately and returned to his task at hand. Ben slowly came back out of the break room to ever cautiously finish his day in the cellar.

CHAPTER 25

As the workload was slowly shrinking, more of us had days off together. Gossip circled around both facilities that soon the majority of our team would be laid off with little notice or remorse from the winery. The Shiraz had all been harvested, and the smaller production lots of Grenache, Mataro and Cabernet Sauvignon were being processed mostly at Marananga, which only required the labor of two people. We got wind that the Two Hands End of Vintage Show was set to happen before Easter. A lot of the temporary team was counting on working the entire month of April and enjoying more civilized eight hour work days at that. Ben didn't deter our fears and conspiracies at all. I wrote a song called "The Branson Blues" about all of these things, which at least made us chuckle about our imminent demise the couple times I played it on my ukulele at break time.

Timmy and I were on the same page to go tasting at as many good wineries as possible before we were given our marching papers. On a rare afternoon off together, he and I headed down to the town of Lyndoch to taste at Burge Family Winemakers, the friend of record studio owner Mick Wordley. We stopped in a bakery that was rumored to have excellent meat pies, and soon drove the long dirt driveway onto the Burge property, which was bordered by the old railroad line and just harvested grapevines. A sign said they were open, but no other cars were around. The tasting room was on the left in a white house with a wrap around porch. We could see a bit of the crush pad and a larger house in back. We opened the creaky door into what could have been the study of an old quaint, wood floored house. Bottles were on display racks, with many different vintages available.

"Hello," a dark haired woman around my age called out as she came out of a back room to the wood bar area. She gave us a look and smile.

"Interested in doing a little tasting?"

"Yes we are," I said as we met her at the bar top. "My friend Mick Wordley sent us your way. I'm Darren."

"Hi Darren, I'm Bailey, and you're not from around here are ya."

"We're both from California. This is Timmy. We're both here working harvest for Two Hands."

I shook her French manicured hand and then she got some glasses out. We tasted a Barossa Semillon first, then got into the Garnacha, Olive Hill, a Mourvédre, then finished with a couple different years of Draycott Shiraz. All of the wines were soulful, not overdone with oak or high alcohol, and Bailey added that they were organically farmed. I was getting into the wines and asking about older vintages, winemaking methods, and Bailey provided every detail with passion. She kept referring to them as "Rick's wines," and raised him up as the finest winemaker in the region.

"Have you had the Two Hands Wines?" I asked her.

"No, but I know Two Hands," she said with a smirk.

"How long have you worked for Rick?"

She spoke about managing the direct sales and cellar doors, and occasionally accompanying Rick on some export visits to Asia. She also did punch downs and helped out with pressing and bottling. Her accent was thickly South Australian, which veers toward Texan, and as each delicious wine crossed my palate and she offered her elaborate and sensual descriptions, I was finding myself drawn to her. No other customers came in as it was a weekday afternoon, so we had her undivided attention, and it seemed only proper to purchase a few wines to go. As usual Timmy wasn't buying, so I asked for a bottle of Olive Hill and an older Draycott Shiraz and started pulling out my wallet.

"Wait. Do you guys like dessert wines?" she asked.

"Sure," we collectively said.

She poured a brown wine that smelled of raspberries, waffles, toffee and milk chocolate. Timmy and I just looked at each other. He started doing his little slightly buzzed jazz shuffle then, since we'd stopped spitting the tastes out second wine in. The wine was called VO and was fortified Grenache mostly aged and oxidized in old barrels, some of the juice spanning ten to twenty years in age. I added that to my order and gave

Bailey my new Australian credit card. She bagged up the wines and we told her about living together in the train car, how harvest was winding down, and that layoffs were on the horizon.

"Did you get to see much of SA?" she asked.

"A little," I said. "Then everything hit and we've been working full on."

"Uh oh Daz," she said. "You've been declined."

"What?"

"Yep," she said with concern. "No good. Got another card?"

If you've ever had your only form of currency denied in a foreign country, you know this naked feeling. Not to mention she and I had been getting slightly flirty, which was surely marred by the unattractive realization of insufficient funds. I'd surely been hacked or ripped off.

"Let's hold off I guess," I said. "Wow, this is embarrassing."

She started teasing me about it, saying something about me likely being homeless, that I probably had never worked for Two Hands, then she said to call back when the card is good and she'll deliver the wines to me.

"Where can I track you down?" she asked me. I wrote down the winery phone number and Matt Wenk's name, and promised to get things sorted on the card.

As we left I knew I'd be crossing paths with Bailey again, and not just financially speaking.

* * *

Calie, Timmy and I hit the Clare Valley the next weekend and tasted at Kilikanoon, Jeanneret, Jim Barry, and Tim Adams, before getting wind of a party thrown by some Saffa cellarhand friend of Calie's. I had brought my guitar and harmonicas just in case. There was a race or festival or something that went down all day in the Clare. The house party became a cool, cultural infusion, with two drunk Christian girls turning up to jam. They harmonized well. One played some worship originals and later inquired as to whether I was a Christian.

"Nah, I used to be. Hey my brother is. Ryan Delmore. You should look up his music."

"But you're not anymore?"

"Me? No."

"Why?"

"I'm still spiritual, I just… feel like I have to try to bring goodness into the world, to make it a better place. It's up to me."

"That's not an easy job."

"No. Not always."

At their insistence and with the lame acoustic in hand, I played a bunch of Cranberries tunes with them, some Fleetwood Mac, and more stuff I never play. One of my more inspired guitar solos inspired a Japanese cellar hand to run home and grab his Didgeridoo. He came back and we jammed till my fingers bled. We talked about vintage, how everyone had been treated, and I asked the Clare Valley based interns what it was like working in this even more remote part of South Australia. Most of them had already booked their post vintage vacations, which I realized I should probably start looking into. Calie and I drank multiple Coopers Pale Ales on the drive home while Timmy drove, which was strange and legal.

* * *

My dreams were getting even wilder. After hiking down a combination of the Presidio area of San Francisco and into a remote Surf Beach like area, a young mother's one year old crawled ahead of me on the metal steps down to the deep sandy beach and flew off and disappeared into the sand. I hit the sand beside the mother as she wailed in horror. I dipped my hand into the granules, feeling for the thing, and after a minute I clutched its fetus-sized belly and pulled the baby boy up out of the sand. "Oh my god!" the mother wailed. Sand filled his nostrils, mouth, eyes, everything. "He's dead!" She screamed. I laid the baby down, felt for a pulse that wasn't there, then administered mouth to mouth. The baby started coughing out handfuls of sand. "It's working," the mother shrieked. I blew into his mouth again and these huge clumps of sand kept coming out of him like he was a little sandbag; finally the last coughs of sand came out and the baby cried and screamed. I placed him in his mother's arms.

CHAPTER 26

After work on Thursday, Fiona turned up at the derailment with my restrung baritone ukulele and even a cell phone and charger for me to have. I knew earlier in the shift that she was coming by to hang out, and Timmy and I decided we should have some kind of signal in the unlikely event of female company onboard. I said I'd leave my cellar boots outside the front door if he had to find alternative accommodations, which I did the moment she arrived. She was dressed in a skirt and stockings and tight button up shirt that showed off her breasts. I immediately cracked a Jeanneret Riesling as we caught up on the bed in the train car. The topic turned to her being sorry how things went the night of my gig there, Clare Valley Riesling versus Eden Valley Riesling, and weed, which she mentioned she has growing out in Eden Valley. She had pot cookies too.

"Do you want to smoke?" I asked her.

"Sure," she said.

I got excited, nearly lighting up in the train.

"Do you smoke in here?" she asked.

I pointed toward the cramped bathroom. "In the shower I do."

She laughed.

"Maybe we could smoke in my car on the way," she proposed.

"Is it music night at the Clubhouse?" I asked.

"Oh yeah, it's Thursday. Let's go and have a drink there."

"And we can smoke after," I pointed out. I grabbed the ukulele and a joint and we walked outside.

"My car smells badly of diesel I'm sorry," she said.

I got in and it was true. "We might ignite this thing if we smoked in here."

We drove to the Clubhouse with windows down, the chilly night air blowing against the fumes. At the Clubhouse, or "the morgue" as the male cellar hands had started calling it, a table of six women made up the clientele for the evening. Half the lights were out. Fiona bought us a round of Pewsey Vale Riesling. The bartender knew her by name.

"Isn't it music night tonight?" I asked.

"Starts next week, mate," he said. "The TH has theirs tonight. It's more electric though. Younger crowd than we get."

We finished our wines and resorted to the car. I lit up as she took the Tanunda backstreets toward the junction, and we passed the joint back and forth till it started burning my fingers. The weed backfired on me. We both got a world class case of cottonmouth, for one thing. Back at the train, Fiona climbed onto my bed right away after asking which bed was mine. I went to the bathroom, coming out to see her sitting on the edge of the bed with a classic stoner glaze on her eyes. She had *Family Guy* playing on the TV. I laid around and brought an arm around her waist. She didn't move. I kept moving closer and started rubbing her back. Nothing. I sat up after the first episode and waited to see any sign that she wanted me to keep doing what I was doing. Nothing. Finally I just went in for a kiss and we kissed gently, in a very dry fashion, through the commercials.

"Do you want a glass of wine?" I asked.

"Nah I've gotta drive."

"How about a glass of water?"

"Cheers. That'd be great darl'."

I'd never been called darl' before, and I have to say, I kind of liked it.

We rehydrated and laughed through the next *Family Guy*. Then I took the empty glass from her and leaned in again and started kissing her. I felt obnoxious, and after that second round of kissing I gave up. The last episode finished up and she said she had to get going. I thanked her at the door for her generosity and planned to play her Tapas night event again on the 16th.

"Bye darl'," she said. I scooted my cellar bottles back inside and closed the door fast behind me to keep the army of moths and mosquitos out.

CHAPTER 27

The Vintage Show, as the higher ups at Two Hands call their annual end of harvest party in Adelaide, roared straight into oblivion. With little notice and conducted on a Saturday while there were still active fermentations going on up in the Barossa, our overworked and grape-stained team was sure to "erupt like a powder keg" as Michael Twelftree put it to Ben. Many factors were to blame for my inebriated downfall, starting with my mistake of getting stoned before indoor go-kart racing ensued. What was supposed to be a lively, team building exercise swiftly turned into an Olympic battle of the continents, and many of us suffered both whiplash and oxygen deprivation. This was followed by the T-Chow long lunch with over 25 epic wines from Michael's personal cellar and a crate of lobsters that he brought for their chef to thrown down with. The wines were mainly from Burgundy and Napa Valley, with a few Australian and Chateauneuf-du-Pape bottles in the mix. Everything was awfully expensive and nicely cellared, and with the amount of hours our team had put in this harvest, such a liquid lunch and feast chucked the mere idea of moderation out the window. After all of this, it was optional to join an open tab fiasco at the Exeter, find and pay for our own lodging in the city, or drive hammered back up to Tanunda.

I emailed Ava the day before and said I'd phone her after the lunch and before the raging bar scene of the Exeter, so that she could join the festivities and I could sleep over, but was so drunk and high it escaped me. Amid the roar of it all, I noticed her sitting at the bar by herself, staring at me. My backpack was on and I'd been strumming my ukulele like a drunken lunatic. Most of my trashed bosses and colleagues had moved on to gin and tonics, but Ben, Gareth and I were drinking heavily off a second bottle of 1999 Greenock Creek Cabernet from the bar's reserve list at $250 a bottle, all on the Two Hands tab. Ben's eyes looked like they'd been placed in a tanning bed for over a week. Gareth was so wasted he kept calling me "gold." Earlier he was screaming for me to "play that Henry Rollins tune," mistakenly meaning the Dave Rawlings Machine song he liked. "What, do you want to hear 'I'm a Liar?'" I kept joking back. We were purple lipped and collectively far gone by this moment of the evening, which was early, and Ava was bummed that I hadn't called her earlier as planned to tell her of my whereabouts, since I was supposed to get her in on the action and stay the night with her.

I somehow made my way over and was earnestly excited and surprised to see her. She was upset that I hadn't called her to tell her it was time to head down to meet up. She'd known we were going to eventually be at the Exeter, but I never rang her. I hadn't even activated the new phone Fiona gave me. Why hadn't I written her cell phone number down on my list of important numbers? Inconsiderate. She told me so and I apologized. I held her hand to walk her over to where I'd been sitting and introduced her to Ben. All of my coworkers started looking my way and cracking up. I apologized to her again and asked "Can I pour you some of this three hundred dollar wine?"

"Take your backpack off, seriously," she advised. I sat it down by my feet, asked the bartender for a wine glass, poured her up, and gave her an overview of what was going on. The highlights had been Michael Rizzo going off on Twelftree and Phil about how pissed off he was regarding the way he was treated during harvest, to which he got a good "get fucked" in return. Somehow that escalated to him and Phil embracing, hugging, kissing on the mouth even, and then dancing around the barroom in each other's arms. Nathan came over and mumbled to her how much of a good dude I was and how she was lucky to be here with me.

"Is that right?" she smirked. He was trashed.

Then Phil of all people surfaced and came over and told her, "You are one hot chick!" He looked at me, almost falling over, and clarified, "Darren you are with a hot chick!" I put a hand on Ava's thigh and told her how happy I was that she was here. Phil spaced out and walked away.

"Uh oh look out," she said all of a sudden with widened eyes. She grabbed my arm and looked behind me. I felt something on the back of my legs. Two cops with a drug sniffing dog had entered the bar and the little beast jumped on my backpack again and started pawing like crazy at it.

"Excuse me sir," I heard an authoritative male voice say, "this is a registered drug sniffing dog, and we have the indication that we need to conduct a search. Will you come with us outside please?"

I really didn't believe it was happening.

"You'll be all right," Ava assured me with made up, worried eyes. Most of my coworkers had gotten wind of what was going down. I brought my backpack outside into the alleyway to face the search.

"Are you carrying anything?" one of the cops asked me.

"A small amount of marijuana," I confessed.

"Will you get it out for me?"

I kneeled down and pulled out the half-ounce bag of weed. He held it up to his light. "He's going to search the rest of your bag," he pointed to the other cop.

The other officer found the other little bag and pipe which I'd forgotten that I'd brought and handed it up to the main cop. Time was at a stand still. I thought I was going down. People were spilling outside onto the street to have a look at me, the cops, and the beagle.

"Okay, I'm going to issue you an on-the-spot fine and citation for this. I won't arrest you. Basically you'll be paying a one hundred and eighty dollar fine. Do you have some identification and place of residence?"

I got out my driver's license and thought of something. "I have a uh, medical prescription in there for marijuana. I'm not sure if it means anything here. I have a condition."

"You do?" The cop was amazed.

"Yeah." I reached into my bag and got out my Dr. Sanzani prescription. The cop held it up to his flashlight and read the whole thing. The other cop, somewhat amused, came in for a look. Suddenly Timmy appeared, standing bravely by my side doing his acid-jazz-dance-groove-when-there's-no-acid-jazz-playing-drunk-thing. Bless his heart. I felt like an asshole for everything I'd put him through. I'd later learn that Ava had absolutely snapped on him and Ben in the bar to go outside and support their mate. Ben came out more cautiously with his pockets in his hands.

"You okay Daz?"

"I think so," I said. He went quickly back inside.

"You're welcome to contest this claim," the cop said, filling out my citation on a little sheet. "Not sure if it'll get you anywhere here."

I gave him the Two Hands winery address for my place of residence and he gave me my ticket. Then he said he was going to ask me a series of questions that I didn't legally have to answer. I forget what they were, but they seemed minor. We parted ways with handshakes and I went back into the Exeter pub to the rowdy cheers of my Two Hands team and Ava's comforting embrace. People were high fiving me and laughing their asses off about all of it, even Phil and Twelftree. I was shaking and slick with sweat. Ava could tell and got me out of there, but not before I ordered one last Greenock Creek Cab and a bottle of Ashton Hills Pinot, putting the full bottle of Pinot directly in the empty spaces of my backpack before she and I ran out unannounced.

A taxi across the city had us sitting safely on her couch in no time. If I was in another part of Australia, I probably would've been in jail or else deported. South Australia was the most lenient state in the country regarding cannabis, which I now knew firsthand. It was only eight o' clock. Soon my shirt was ripped off of me and we were at it. I undressed her on the couch and she clenched my hand and rushed us up to her bedroom.

In the dim morning light, we had sex again, then I rushed to get ready for the morning bus, drinking handfuls of water from the bathroom tap. She dropped me at the bus station at 8:45. "That was all a bit fast," she remarked as we kissed goodbye.

The bus ride north wasn't long enough to even remotely contemplate the last 24 hours. I listened to Gillian Welch and The Band, and took in the scenery as things went from urban sprawl to ag lands, laughing about the events of the evening and occasionally trying to write it all down in my journal. You could say I was a happy man, there on that bus, living in one of those rare, fleeting good moments of life. I was lucky. I had an easy afternoon half shift at Maranaga to get to, but enough time to get coffee and clean myself up beforehand.

Then things actually got even better. I checked my email and Facebook at the café and discovered that Bailey, the woman that poured wine for Timmy and me at Burge Family Winemakers the week beforehand, wanted to have me over for dinner, and that tonight was the only night she could do it because of child custody issues. I'd chatted with her online one night after meeting her, flirting some for sure, but didn't think she'd really want to get together with a random Californian whose credit card got declined when she swiped it. Apparently I was wrong. I blinked at the idea at first, thought it was totally insane in the state I was in, though she baited me with opening multiple vintages of the wine I liked best at their cellar door: Olive Hill. Burge Family produced phenomenal wines, wines that the producer Mick Wordley had recommended on his scribbled note months beforehand at the Wheatsheaf Hotel. Yes, I was in.

Matt and I laughed about everything that happened at the End of Vintage show later that day. We were pressing off some tanks that shift, with no incoming fruit to crush since it was a skeleton crew Sunday. Timmy had apparently shit his bed in the train car while Gareth slept nearby. Phil had drunkenly left the bar without closing out the tab, and the remaining casuals ran the bill up into the thousands. Many had puked. Some had tried and failed to drive back to the Barossa. I mentioned how I had met Bailey and that she was picking me up from Marananga to cook me dinner that night at her house in the Barossa and open a vertical of Olive Hill.

"Whoa mate. Three in three?" Matt exclaimed around the press.

"Oh man… Just about. I guess you're right." I forgot about telling Matt about the Fiona date in the train car, which hadn't amounted to anything anyway.

Matt cracked a giggle and looked up at the sky, holding his palms up at it, as if God was smiling down on me, and he was catching a residual, lucky ray of light.

Unrested, I did what I could to be productive at work. I juggled pump overs while a full press load was in the basket. I was supposed to be cleaning myself up for the night's adventures but work took precedence until Michael Rizzo and Timmy turned up for the shortened night shift at 6:15. I used the Two Hands shower while a tied up pump over was circulating Grenache that scented the entire fermentation hall with wild strawberries and white pepper. As I returned up top to finish the job, I saw a dark blue BMW pull up and stop by the press where Michael Rizzo stood. As Michael and the driver chatted, I jammed to push water through so I could at least get changed into non-grape stained clothing. Bailey confused Rizzo with me, asking if he was ready. He thought she was someone who worked at the Two Hands cellar door.

"Are we doing some tasting or something?" he asked her.

"I thought we'd sorted dinner out," she said.

"Oh. We're doing dinner?" a probably still drunken Michael asked.

"You're not Darren, are you," she finally figured out.

"Oh! You're looking for Darren Delmore!" he exclaimed.

As I got out of the bathroom Michael and Timmy filed in.

"So who's the hot mom out there for you in the parking lot?" Michael said with a high pitched, teasing tone.

"She's here, huh?"

"She thought you were me," Michael said.

I went into the lab to find Matt and get the early exit OK.

"She's out there in a BMW," I added.

"With tinted windows?" Matt asked, laughing.

"I think so. Is that cool if I get going early?"

"Yeah. If you don't root her I'll be fucking pissed," Matt said.

"I'll do my best."

I walked out with Matt and saw Bailey idling by the old vines. She waved out the window.

"Ah okay," Matt said, amused and hung over himself.

"See ya at two tomorrow," I said.

"Sure that's enough time, mate?" he joked.

She stepped out of the vehicle and motioned for me to put my ukulele and backpack in the backseat. She was wearing a button up and jeans that flaunted her leggy stature. Two Hands tongues were wagging as I was whisked away to a working class town called Gawler.

With hip-hop on the system, we chatted and got to know each other a bit. I clarified my credit card fiasco as a result of not properly activating it before the visit to the Burge cellar door, which she partially believed. She talked herself up as one of the strongest female figures on the Australian wine scene, a role that didn't form many new friendships with women or men. "I just do my thing." She spoke of her sales trip to Hong Kong with Rick Burge, the dinners and tastings they'd conduct, how he'd open wine from his cellar all the time for her, and how Rick's wife is beautiful and blonde.

After tasting through the wines at Burge, I first thought Bailey was Bailey Burge. She knew the wines, knew what went into them, and presented them with sincere pride and admiration for the man who made them.

After a twenty minute drive, we pulled up to her Hill Street cottage and parked in an ancient narrow garage. There was a small dark blue car already backed into it with a for sale sign on the windshield. "Now, I have a dog, and she snores louder than any man alive."

"Good to know."

Her dog Holly was a small, crusty, sweet thing and she greeted us at the door. Her single level house, like many in the Barossa, was old, but beautifully maintained with wood floors and spacious nooks here and there. I was surprisingly loose around her so far. Maybe the fact that I was guaranteed a guest room status and that anything else would take some work and effort on my part eased some tension. She was going to cook me dinner, open Burge Olive Hill reds from 2001-2004, and even offered to make me breakfast in the morning.

She brought in a half box of wine from her car and placed the Olive Hill on the kitchen table, lined up by vintage. Beneath them were three 1971 Tawny Port bottles from Shiraz grown in McLaren Vale—bought at auction on Langton's for $210 a 6 pack.

"So, are you ready for a drink or what?" she asked.

"Absolutely," I said with a smile.

In a lab beaker turned decanter, she poured the 2001 and soon we were having a glass. After giving it a swirl, I started asking her Burge winemaking and farming questions. Rick Burge had been included in Robert Parker's "World's Greatest Wine Estates" book that I had back home, and although the wines were impossible to find in America, his organically farmed, naturally fermented wines were full of character and some of the finest I'd had in Australia thus far. She lit a cigarette and I followed her outside. The 2001 was dangerously delicious, like Bailey was becoming with every sip. She moved gracefully, crossed her long legs as she smoked like a debutante, sizing me up, proud of her work, exhaling clouds of smoke and responding with a matter of fact sass to every question. With beautifully resolved tannins, loaded with fruit and game, richness and pure pleasure, the 2001 was better than the 2005 that I'd tried to buy in the tasting room before getting my card declined, though that wine should become like this in time.

"I'm supposed to be cooking you dinner!" she laughed as the last of the beaker was poured out in less than thirty minutes. "Are you alright?"

"I'm wonderful," I said. "I brought a Pinot along if you want to try it in the mix."

We went inside and I pulled the bottle out of my backpack. The Ashton Hills had zesty red and purple fruit notes, refreshing acidity, and a dreamy, lengthy finish. Bailey absolutely loved it and took a picture of the bottle with her phone.

"Would you like a sous chef tonight?" I finally offered.

She laughed and said "you can toss the salad." Things were heating up indeed. I drained the glass of Pinot and poured myself the 2002 Olive Hill which was incredible and a little more advanced than the 2001. I got to work on drunkenly chopping lettuce and veggies by her sink. Once completed, I asked her how it looked and she said, "Um, sure, I can do rustic."

"Rustic? Oh man."

"It'll do, Daz."

"Can I put on some music?" I started talking up the artist Cat Power, who she hadn't heard of before. We headed over to her computer so I could click on a couple Cat Power tunes. She downloaded "The Greatest" and started playing the album.

A quick dinner of lamb, yogurt, couscous and salad accompanied a more feral 2003 Olive Hill, which Bailey didn't much care for. "Obviously there are years left to it, but it's just not quite there at the moment." My stomach flared up, so I cleared my plate and brought it to the sink.

"Just leave it there, 'cause you'll be washing these in the morning."

We were pretty smashed at this point. She brought her plate up to the sink and washed her hands. "Come," she said, "play me something on that toy you have."

"You wanna hear it?" I said.

"Outside, so I can smoke."

We sloppily filled our glasses with the black colored 2004 Olive Hill and made our way outside. There was a slight breeze and enough warmth to balance it out. We sat opposite each other on the covered benches, and I started picking Spanish flamenco style on my ukulele. Then I went into "Black and Brown Blues" by the Silver Jews, "In the Reins" by Iron and Wine, and Bailey brought her feet up on the small bench with a cigarette and relaxed while I strummed and picked a Lemonheads song. When I finished up, she smiled and said that I had a natural gift and talent, how I was absolutely lovely and that she could listen all night. She was staring at me with glossy eyed intent, blowing each puff of smoke out with elegance. We migrated into her living room area where her dog was snoring up a storm and we laughed about it. She turned up Cat Power and we sat beside each other on the couch and talked about her ex who broke her finger in a rage, how she'll go out now and then "to pick up with my girlfriends," how she slept with a woman when she was in her 20's, and some Irish guy she fucked recently and sent on his way. She reiterated how she doesn't shag winemakers.

"Lucky me," I quipped. "So I'd have to be a rowdy obnoxious Irish man to get down with you then?"

"Aw give it a crack," she said.

We drank more of the 2004 and she said, "Shall we get into the 1971?"

"Really? That'd be unreal."

I followed her into the kitchen, standing beside her as she tampered with the foil on the Hardy's, and then she stopped, turned and grabbed me and we started kissing. My fantasy was now complete. I returned the passion and she moaned. She took my hand and said "come on" and marched me down the hall. We nearly collapsed on the way and I slammed into the wall hard. I started to undo her buttons and she stopped me, doing it herself. She ripped off my long sleeve shirt as we tumbled onto her bed.

Her dog's snores thundered the cottage all night, and mine too apparently. In the morning I held her from behind and started feeling her legs and hips, and ultimately started touching the smooth underside of her breasts. When I lightly felt her nipples she gasped. I continued the motion until she shuddered and moaned. Then I got on top of her and she stroked me as I gripped her breasts and sucked on her neck. Assured, I glided myself inside of her. I had to stop myself, breathe, and go again over the course of ten minutes until we came together.

"Are you okay," she asked as I gasped and trembled, still inside of her.

I must have sounded like I was having a cardiac arrest. I nodded, sweating and shaking. "Coffee," she said. I passed out straight away.

I was still out an hour later when she said, "I could use a shower." I watched her naked body leave the room then fell asleep again. She woke me up and I eventually went for a shower, slowly coming to my senses underneath the warm stream. I heard the door open and Bailey came in. "You sing in the shower too, eh?" she said.

"Yep." I wasn't even aware I was doing it.

"Just grabbing a brush."

I came out in a towel and saw her starting to wash last night's dishes. "Leave those for me, Bailey. I promised."

"Okay, okay."

I got dressed as she smoked a cigarette. I tackled the dirty load with a restaurateur's precision. "I like the way you do that," she commented. "Now I'm going to make more dishes for you to wash." She opened up a package of thick Aussie bacon, sizzled the strips up, fried eggs next, and served them on some toast with coffee.

When we finished, she announced, "Now it's time to get some jumpers for your new car."

"Car?" I asked with a confused look on my face.

"Ha! I just shit myself! Ha! Yes, right. I've decided to give you my car. Battery is dead. We'll go get the jumpers though, then you can actually get around and come see me again." She was giving me a car. What was happening here?

"Are you kidding?"

"Nah Daz. I wish I could see your Two Hands mates' faces when you pull up in a car I gave ya! Haha!"

We drove to an auto parts store in Gawler and went in together, with her running the show. As she put the cables on the counter I intervened with my credit card.

"I'm at least paying for these," I said, putting out my Visa card.

"Sure that'll work?" she hissed.

"You've got a point."

Back at her house, while charging my new ride, I found out the old blue Mazda I was inheriting had a battery too dead for even jumper cables.

The for sale sign taped to the window was asking $800. She called a friend for advice while I tinkered on a piano that was in the garage by the car.

"You love your music, huh?" she commented. "Come on, off again!"

We returned to the auto parts store for a new battery. "Welcome to Bailey's world," she said in the parking lot. "If I want something, I buy it." She took her dead battery out herself.

"I'm a disgrace to my gender," I said while she cranked it out, "and awfully aroused."

At the shop, when I lifted the matching new battery off the shelf, I tipped what looked like water but was battery acid onto my bare arm.

"Careful there," the feral dude at the reg said. "That stuff will burn right through your clothes and your skin." I put it on the counter and noticed the slight burning sensations.

"You're putting this one back in Daz, and there will be a test," she said. I laughed, yet was nervous with the assignment.

With her help, I did put it back together. The Mazda fired up beautifully. She was funny, she did a full safety check: blinkers, break lights, wipers, fluids and water levels. She filled it up with water. "Keep an eye on this for me," she warned.

"There are three Baileys" I remembered her telling me one night while chatting online. "The Bailey you met at Burge, Bailey the mum of two boys, and then the real Bailey." I was seeing a combination of the latter two here.

I gave her a kiss and she hugged me, holding on even tighter. I thanked her for her generosity and told her I couldn't wait to see her again. Off I drove, through blue collar Gawler, with pure joy creasing up my face, like I'd gotten away with something incredible.

When I pulled into the parking lot at Marananga that afternoon, almost everyone stopped production when they saw me step out. Matt was the most impressed and Timmy was mad. It took me to a different level of respect around Two Hands.

CHAPTER 28

On Monday morning we got the official word on Two Hands letterhead about the upcoming layoffs, and that a few cellar casuals would be offered two extended weeks of work but at a lower hourly pay rate with no overtime. Ben told me in private that I was one of those offered an extension. I agreed, as I'd planned on working until the end of April anyway, and needed the money if I was going to take a surf trip up the Gold Coast before flying home. Most of my teammates were angry about it and clamoring amongst themselves about how screwed we were getting. I still felt like it was a fair deal, in comparison to the no frills harvest gigs I'd worked in the past.

Wednesday night, a black lipped, blurry-eyed, and flirty Michael Rizzo vented to me at Marananga about sticking to his principles and leaving Two Hands, even though they offered him an extension, since they did him wrong. Then he accused me for taking their "fist up my ass" for two more weeks of work.

"Hey," I said from atop the forklift, "I set a financial goal. I have a criminal violation to pay off now. I'll make five hundred a week for two more weeks and be where I need to be."

"And where is that?"

I turned the forklift off finally, as he'd been trailing me around the barrel hall slurring his frustrations while I was trying to stack full barrels of wine in a line. "With six-thousand bucks."

"You will make six grand from Two Hands?" He held his mouth open in shock. Getting into Australia late and quitting early had Rizzo in the negative pay bracket. I clarified to him how I'd been paid late because of the visa hang-ups, and spent three grand of my own while I was here, so it was like I'd have only half of that to leave with.

"Come travel with me Darren!" he yelled. "Fuck Two Hands! Quit!"

"I need to stay," I said.

"It'd be so much better to travel with someone! When you travel alone you have to rent a car so there's thirty a day, then a place to stay, that's like sixty bucks."

I was starting to feel lame for doing my job, but also uncomfortable in the presence of a very drunk man. He'd been over at Rocland with Nathan all shift just drinking from the hogsheads while Nathan did all the work.

"I'm on vacation since like three days ago!" he announced.

"You know man, my recent adventures are blurring my take on everything," I said.

"Oh, you mean all the pussy?!"

"Well, yeah."

"Yeah well if I was getting dick I'd be different too. But there's no dick in Tanunda. See, I need to go to it. I need to find it."

I think that settled things, or painted a clearer picture of where I was at. Calie was apparently seeking legal counsel against Two Hands, Chelsea was chapped and wasting time at every opportunity, and here I had a new phone, new car, some great sex and generous company, and I saw five hundred bucks a week pay as a way to keep it all flowing.

Michael started slamming his fist into a hogshead and screamed, "There's no dick in the Barossa!"

* * *

With Timmy and Kim among the casuals who weren't offered additional work, I made arrangements to move into Nathan's house after the weekend. It was going to cost me merely a hundred bucks a week, which was somehow less than the fucked train car with another man. I announced the new digs to Timmy and within a millisecond he said, "Maybe I'll just crash on your couch then and move out too." This kid didn't miss a scrappy beat.

"It's not my couch and not my say man; it's Nathan's."

With Timmy not able or willing to pay for the entire train car, we were set to move out the next morning, which was Friday, and honestly I couldn't have cared less where Timmy had to go. I had the "Tappers" show to play music at in Angaston that night, and then a farewell party for Kim at Nathan's house afterward. I was prepared to crash in my new Mazda all weekend. I still wanted to head south and surf the famed Knight's Beach in Port Elliot before it was all said and done. There was also the chance to play and record some music with Mick Wordley at his Mixmasters Studio in Adelaide too, which had come up through emailing back and forth. The possibilities were endless with my newfound transportation and actual two day weekends off.

I emailed Ava and offered to take her out to a swanky Adelaide spot called Apothecary for dinner on Saturday, wherein I could possibly fit in a Knight's Beach surf Sunday morning before heading back up to move in to Tanunda that night, once Kim was officially moved out. I was set to be living right on the main drag in Barossa now, in something other than a haunted train car. It would be interesting to have a new living situation, even if only for a couple weeks. Sleeping on Timmy's shit-stained mattress and awaking to his four bowls of cereal smacking noises had been real and all, but the train's mosquitos and possible bed bugs had been grinding me raw, and the dreams... maybe our collective dreamscape was the focal area of the haunting. Never had I been faced with such abstract and time-fetching sleep time scenarios, when all I needed every night was a blank, deep sleep to repair myself.

* * *

The soon-to-be slimmed down Two Hands team had an educational tour of Seppeltsfield Winery that Friday afternoon. Its ancient gravity flow cement tanks and aromas of over a hundred years of fermentations made things seem more museum-like than winery. This was the historic producer we'd been driving by every day and night with its row of Beverly Hills palm trees sticking out of the brown landscape, and claim to fame of a Tawny port called Para, released after a hundred years of barrel aging. We had a seated tasting down in the reserve room, where we tasted the Para with their wine educator. The room was appropriately musty and cavern like, the long table adorned with an ancient, purple felt skirt. The wine was actually green and black in color it was so old. Matt told us to pay attention to the glass after we sipped, that the residual body clinging to the glass hauntingly replenishes the pour. It was true. Once the ounce pour was gone and five minutes had gone by, another ounce appeared.

We congregated up in the cellar door and tried a bevy of their newer dry wines, and with the high proof alcohol in all of us, I noticed Timmy doing the acid-jazz gyration movements he does when he's buzzed. Tales of his bed defecation the night of the end of vintage show had made it through the entire staff, so I mentioned out loud, "Timmy, the toilet in the men's room is broken but they put a nice mattress in there for the meantime."

* * *

I played another mediocre gig at Barossa Collective to the half amused group of drunks and for the same no-pay, no-bottles payment as before. Fiona wanted me to stay afterward but I had a party to go to at my new house. I wasn't going to play into her situation anymore and said a simple "so long." It felt good leaving.

"I'll bring some good booze," Matt had promised earlier in the day regarding the party and he came through with it. This was more of a farewell party to some of the interns who were being laid off and sent on their way. I drove the Mazda from Angaston to Tanunda with a sack of chips, and as I pulled up saw some familiar vehicles out front, including Heintje's motorcycle. I came in with Ben's guitar to a packed, jovial living room and tons of beers opened on the coffee table. I'd brought a nearly full priced Radford 2007 Shiraz and set it on the table, going straight away toward a glass of 2004 Alice's from Greenock Creek. Ben came right over to harass me for starting my evening off with it. "All A.P. John's, all reshaved," he said, laughing about the iconic winery's traditional use of the Aussie cooper.

"Is the guy a cheap bastard?" I asked, smelling the glass.

He nodded. I liked the ripe slightly bretty wine with its polished tannins and character. I could barely look at Timmy who was enjoying all the free drinks and amenities, and no doubt planning on staying here now that we'd officially moved out. "I need to be more patient with him," I thought to myself, while at the same time feeling the urge to chuck a full bottle of Cooper's Sparkling Ale at this face from across the room. I wondered if I'd miss him when he was gone. Most likely not.

Heintje was there like a lazy, patient boa constrictor in a large cage, with a drunken Kim—his weary mouse to at some point devour. His head was recently shaved to the scalp and no one was talking to him, so I chatted with him a bit. Throughout the course of vintage, I kind of liked him. He never stressed out, he knew how the equipment worked, and he earnestly wanted to be friends with us. His work ethic got criticized by Ben and Nathan, but in reality, he was having the vintage of his lifetime thanks to hooking up with Kim. Can't blame a man for being sidetracked by lust and pangs of possible love.

I moved on and sat by Ben and his fiancée Megan on the couch. Matt put on these oversized green party glasses and started smiling at everyone. Timmy and Calie bailed for the bar in search of mythical women. I remembered the Radford and headed into the kitchen for a glass of water first, when I got busted for my big mouth by Kim, who came in to tell me how upset she was that I suggested to Nathan that she sanitize my future bedroom with caustic and citric acid before I moved in, like a wine tank. The restaurateur in me smoothed that one over quick and I hugged and apologized for the joke.

"Everyone makes stupid jokes about that kind of stuff about people who have sex somewhere."

Mere moments later I was laughing while Ben suggested I take a UV light to both the bed and the couch. Heintje heard us, and his grin suggested he was kind of proud about it. Back in the living room, the iPod died and I picked up the guitar and harmonica and started playing "Caroline" by Old Crow Medicine Show. Kim leaned back and relaxed while Matt Wenk looked over beaming, since he'd never heard me actually play. Feeling the booze, I went into an audience participation set of "I Won't Back Down," "Patience" by Guns and Roses, and R.E.M.'s "The One I Love." Chelsea's boyfriend James asked for my harmonica, so I reluctantly chucked it over to him and warned that he should run it through a Planned Parenthood first before blowing on it.

"That is so wrong," Michael Rizzo said, who'd been drinking heavily but fairly quiet all night.

"Michael, I can do 'Careless Whisper' if you can," I suggested.

"I'm not drunk enough for that," he said with a shrug.

Ben went into a rowdy traditional Australian song with the verse, "I'd like to have a beer with Darren! I'd like to have a beer with Daz!" Then he forgot the rest of the words.

As we winded down a little and Matt got up to leave, I started playing "Just What I Needed" by The Cars. He stopped and shrieked, "Is that what I think it is? Fuck! That's my music!"

Everyone joyously sang along. Matt took off afterward and the house cleared out. Nate went to sleep, leaving me, Kim and Heintje the boa out there to feed. I gave sleeping in my car in the driveway a try, but then said screw it and came inside and took the couch. Kim gave me a pillow and a blanket. I fell asleep fast with a full glass of Radford and dark chocolate on the table. At some point in the night I realized I wasn't alone, and that Timmy was on the couch too, our heads inches apart. We had a tugging battle with the blanket, which prompted me to move to the opposite side of the couch, repulsed.

CHAPTER 29

In the morning, after changing and brushing my teeth, I drove to Blond Coffee, hoping Gareth would turn up to hang out as planned. My life was packed into my car, but no bubbling carboy of homemade wine this time around. After a half hour or so, I headed to the farmer's market to pick up some fruit and charcuterie for my road trip south.

I drove on into the heart of Adelaide to see Ava, and that's when all the grandeur I'd been showered with came to an end. The Mazda started overheating and ultimately died in the middle of the red light district in a center lane, amid a sea of pissed off taxis and traffic. A man and two cops pushed me out of the frenzy and, not having a working cell phone, I called Ava from the Hudsons Coffee phone. I kept pouring water into the radiator, filling up my water bottle six times in the café. Most of it poured right out of the cracked thing. Ava bailed me out like a professional, arranging a tow to her house.

She saved me, showing up streetside a short while later in jeans with a black N.W.A. t-shirt on. She hugged me and hung on tight, assuring me with her red lipstick smile that everything was fine. Before we knew it we were back at her flat, with the Mazda safely in a parking spot to be dealt with the next day. The stress of it all and my sweaty, red-faced embarrassment had evaporated, thanks to Ava's calming vibes. After catching up on her couch and talking about her wine bar, my upcoming move to a civilized rented room, and the status of my criminal violation from the last time we'd seen each other, it was practically time to get dressed for our dinner booking at Mesa Lunga on Gouger Street. The Apothecary was apparently closed for a private party, so she'd chosen Mesa Lunga as a nice alternative.

We took a taxi to the stylish, street corner Tapas spot that proved to be a romantic domain, especially in light of a bottle of Arneis from Adelaide

Hills and my springing for a bottle of Clarendon Hills Grenache. We migrated from the bar to a small table in the corner where we started making out. I noticed people staring and eventually pointing and laughing at our unbridled public affection, so I toned it down a bit and we finished our glasses. We closed out and she led us to the Grace Emily Hotel for a beer and even trashier public displays of affection out back, before bringing it back home.

* * *

On Monday morning I called in to Matt and told him of the vehicle situation. Ava then called me a tow truck. It took a lot longer to get a tow here than it did in California. She arranged for it to be worked on by a mechanic in the Grace Emily family known as "Chopper," who had a garage in the city and a massive belly. When we got there, I shook his hand firmly and he winced in pain.

"Oh I'm sorry," I said.

"Nah mate. I dislocated my shoulder yesterday," he clarified, scowling at me.

This isn't a good start, I thought, fearing a thousand dollar repair.

Ava and I left to run some of her errands for her business, and went for coffee in Norwood, feeling like I used to with my mom in a way. She and I formulated a plan to do a set of music at the Grace Emily that night for what they call Billy Bob's BBQ—their version of an open mic. Her phone rang and it was Chopper with great news. The car was fixed for $160. A blown series of hoses was all it was. She offered to spot me until I could withdraw the cash and pay her back. We picked up the car and I chugged back to Ava's for the Italian dinner she was going to make us. I finally lost my musical nerve and played her some songs. She played me an old soul song called "Jealous Guy," then tried to get me to learn the Tom Waits song "Down in a Hole."

We dressed up and went down to a packed scene at the Grace Emily. First order was getting on the performance list. I didn't have a guitar but brought my harmonicas and a capo, holding it all outside in my hand as we waited to get in. Once inside the bar area, we bumped into indie rockers, punkers, dreadlocked dudes, cowgirls and cowboys all raging alongside each other in the bar and stage area. The first band started up with Billy Bob himself front and center wearing jeans, a wife beater, and a massive cowboy hat. Ava's violent ex-boyfriend was apparently up there on guitar and looked just like a friend of mine from back home, who looks like me. A group of Ava's friends turned up later who were super nice individuals. She took me out back where the jokey hot dog BBQ was happening and introduced me as "Darren from California" to Billy Bob. He jotted my name down for a later fifteen-minute slot. That made me nervous, in light of the diversity of attendees. "He played the Wheaty," she clarified to Bob.

"Do you have an acoustic I can use?" I asked.

"There'll be one lying around I'm sure," he said.

Knowing I'd be getting up there in front of more than a hundred talented people, I started drinking faster. Plowed through four Cooper's Sparkling ales like it was Evian. A punk band was on stage, raging with distortion and manic drums. More people flooded in the entrance, causing loud, shoulder to shoulder capacity. Billy Bob came over and let me know I'd be up after the next band and that he had a nylon string classical guitar for me.

"Following these guys?" I asked.

"You'll be right, mate," he said with a wink.

I flopped a potential set list around in my mind. "Do you want a stage beer?" Ava asked me, seeing the fear in my face, and pulled out some cash.

"I better."

When she returned with the bottle of Coopers Pale Ale, I gripped it hard enough to nearly shatter it into pieces. The punk rock twenty year olds were tight up there, and a mosh pit started up in front. There hadn't been a single solo performer all night. As they finished up, Billy Bob took the mic.

"Okay, okay. Let's hear it for Darren. He came all the way over from California to play here tonight!"

Everything blurred as I moved up onstage into the lights. Ava and her friends were front and center, screaming and clapping. I put a C harmonica into my neck holder and got the guitar around me. "Thanks Billy Bob. I've got a couple songs here, uh, for ya." I started with "In the Reins" by Iron and Wine and Ava was loving it, shouting in approval there. I lost the sweatier part of the audience, but as I opened my eyes on the final verse, the barroom was packed again. When I finished, the applause was beyond what I'd ever gotten out of any little show back home. This crowd was made of music lovers and I thankfully wasn't getting flipped off or drinks chucked at me. I played "Pancho and Lefty" next with a harmonica sola, then finished with "Sunken Waltz" by Calexico and forgot a part at the end. I started to leave and Billy Bob yelled out for another. I played a sweet song called "Black and Brown Blues" by Silver Jews to close it, and as I got off stage, Billy Bob gave me an enthusiastic handshake and two drink tickets for doing a decent job.

A leather adorned, Vegas-sideburned dude and his band took the stage for a couple rowdy rock n' roll jams before the house band came back on around midnight. I grabbed a drink for Ava and another beer with the tickets. Her friends and I were nudging her to sing. She apparently had a gig in a couple weeks and hadn't performed on stage for three years, but finally got up and laid down a powerhouse performance of "Hard to Handle." To my right, one of the punk rock kids nudged me and said, "I bet you're gonna give her a stiff one tonight, eh?"

Ava then sang "Jealous Guy" and was pure soul diva with the house band. Billy Bob, on the guitar, was laughing at how good it all was. She got off stage to rowdy hoots and hollers and her friends and I took turns hugging her. Her guy friend was tearing up, blown away by both of us.

"Man!" he said, looking at me, "you were like Townes Van Zandt, and Ava, you were like Joe Cocker!"

"Fuck you!" Ava retaliated.

We went outside to say bye to her friends and take a taxi to her place, feeling elated by performing. At her place we started kissing on the couch and she climbed on top of me. Then we went upstairs to what soured into an emotional moment full of Ava's tears over her being "just a holiday girl."

"I've never been one before and this is… it's weird. So weird. It's weird. I wish you would like me enough to want to, to take this further. I have zero baggage. But I want you to know that tonight my friends, where I've taken you, all of this is because I think you are cool. That's the only reason why cool stuff happened to you over here." She was crying. I was trying not to say anything stupid or promising. I felt like a drunken monster then, or a real vagabond even. Like my secret was out. She then said she'd written a song about us.

"Are you going to sing it at the Wheatsheaf show?" I drunkenly asked. Her return to gigging was set for a week from Sunday, and she'd invited me to it.

"No! I'm not that pathetic," she said, burying her face in the pillow.

There would be no love making. I passed out on my own side of the bed, then woke up early the next morning to drive back to the Barossa for work. She was sleeping face down. I hugged her goodbye and she hummed her way into it. On the drive up I tried to make sense of the bittersweet weekend, and vowed to leave her alone. She deserved something better, or at least, somebody ready for something real.

CHAPTER 30

I shared my mixed emotions about these recent relations with Chelsea as she ran alcohols in the lab. Some of our finishing alcohols were coming in at 17 percent and higher, which was approaching Port wine levels. Chelsea reckoned she'd feel embarrassed if she was Ava and say so, and that I pay too much mind to female tears. "Girls cry all the time, D.D." she assured me.

"Really?"

"You're looking into it too much," she said, emptying out the test tubes into the sink. "It's vintage."

My reaction had me plotting an immediate withdrawal from seeing Ava. I realized Bailey was more practical about things. I couldn't picture her crying over me. Did that mean she was emotionally shut down? Cold as ice? Or equally as excited about some fun, non-committal company like me?

I got to work on pump overs of some of the remaining fermentations at Marananga, which included late ripening varieties such as Grenache, Mataro, Cabernet, and Barbera. There was still plenty to be done, but without the interns, it seemed a bit strange and slow paced. The team's focus was to finish up everything at Branson and return to operating solely out of Marananga. The amount of fruit flies in the cellar was out of control. It's known to happen at the end of harvest season, where the bugs settle on the sweetest tanks as the sugars push to dryness. On one rectangular tank of Mataro in particular, a twenty minute pumpover required putting on a paint mask to keep them from flying up my nostrils or down my mouth.

That afternoon an unexpected two tons of Mataro for Michael's own new Twelftree label turned up. All the same, Michael, Phil and Matt raved about the quality of what we all made this vintage. There was quantity and quality, with plenty of rich, high octane wines to combine with more elegant lots in their finished blends. The wines were already full of color, flavor and power, and were a high step above the previous five vintages here. However, we thought we were done, with most of the equipment already sanitized and pressure washed to be put to sleep for the season, and here we were scrambling to get it back in place to crush one last micro lot.

With a much smaller crew, there was still a lot of work to do, but a lot less pressure and more regularly plotted work hours. When you work so hard and long, and then find yourself with free hours after work suddenly, you can get bored fast or spiral out of control. I assumed the role of the merry prankster, and that Tuesday night Gareth and I were invited over for dinner at Ben's parents' house in Greenock. His mom was excited to have visitors from other countries. They eradicated the furball of a cat for my allergy's sake, and Ben opened a menthol-laden, silky Oracle Shiraz by Kilikanoon. His parents were chatty with their thick accents, Ben's dad chilling in his leather recliner with the TV on, his mom visiting with Gareth and I on the couch. She made casserole and ate and drank off plates and cups of China. Ben was engaged to be married and had moved back in here after his university days. We'd teased him about living with his folks all vintage, but he didn't really seem to care. But now that we were inside his family's place, he seemed a touch sensitive about it, and kept telling us to move on when we continually brought up his age and digs.

And then I zeroed in on the two framed university portraits of Ben hanging up on the wall. Freshmen year, frosted, and touched up. The best particular shot was Ben in his first year of Uni in a geeky blue sweater and an even more alternative pose, looking like one half of Tears for Fears, or Wham! even. I couldn't stop looking at it, then Gareth and I started laughing.

"Get fucked," Ben said, taking it off the wall and stashing it in the game room. The evening wore on. The Oracle was like morphine-dusted Christmas spice cake and blacking us out by the minute. By midnight Gareth and I had to go, as it was a work night after all. I grabbed my backpack and got my chilled groceries out of their refrigerator, then Ben led us into the game room. I saw the portrait there, resting against the TV. As Ben turned his head to look at something, I jacked it and put it in my backpack out of view, and got it out the door. As Gareth dropped me off at my car in front of Branson, I said, "Get a load of this," and showed the framed portrait to him.

Two days later I asked Shannon at the cellar door to scan it for me, and he emailed me a jpeg and even printed out color wallet-sized versions. I signed a full-sized one to Chelsea from Ben, with "All the best" on it in cursive, and stashed it in the second drawer of the lab desk. I hung the original in Matt Wenk's office next to his kids' framed photos. Ben showed up and went to get something out of the lab drawer and saw it. He came into the break room as I was making coffee and took me by the collar. I lied and said Gareth took a camera picture of it and I printed that out. Later on, I plastered the pic on everyone's Facebook pages, including the Two Hands company Facebook, which actually got a decent amount of likes. Word got out. Meanwhile the framed original still hung in Matt's office upstarts, awaiting his presence on Friday morning. Even Michael Twelftree loved it. By Friday morning Ben had to pull me aside for a drive and express his discontent with the whole ordeal. His voice had that saddened smoker's gravel touch to it. "Why the fuck did you put that on the company website?" he demanded. "It's unprofessional. It doesn't belong there. You go through there and it's just a picture without any writing, anything. I want you to remove it!"

We were having this chat in the company truck, and he was trembling and tearing up. I apologized and started to feel a bit sad. Guess it was too much. The kettle calling the coffee black I think was the saying around here. Ben loved to humiliate others, and here everyone was finally laughing at him. "Your Australian teasing culture has grown on me," I pointed out. I cracked a few jokes on the tense drive over to Branson to soften things up and he said, "Darren you don't have to try hard."

"I bet I won't get my twenty bucks from you now for the charcuterie."

"No," he affirmed.

By Friday afternoon we were getting on well.

CHAPTER 31

I couldn't join Gareth and the crew for a final pint on his last Friday of work because I was hosting Bailey at 7 Murray Street for dinner and overnight shenanigans. Now that I was a bonafide renter of an actual private room, I felt it'd be fair to return the hospitality in what little way I could. Plus, my roommates would be out at the bar for most of the night. I drove to the Tanunda butcher, Foodland, and Tanunda Cellars for a bottle of Kalleske Rosina Old Vine Grenache rosé. I marinated and seasoned the rib-eye steaks, bagged and refrigerated them, then got cleaned up just in time for her arrival. She turned up at 5:50.

"Welcome to my world," I said at the door, a phrase I'd learned from her.

"I brought the entrée," she reminded me, so I helped carry in a box filled with food and wine. She was wearing a high skirt, showing off her legs and pumps. She brought a Louis Latour Chablis La Chanfleure, a Ninth Island Tasmanian Pinot Noir, 2001 Burge Family Olive Hill and a bottle of 2004 Draycott Shiraz. It was on. We started with Chablis as she prepped the smoked salmon, egg, red onion and homemade mayo first course, taking a call from Rick Burge himself all the while. I was a bit star struck by the man who I hadn't met yet, and felt giddy about him being somewhat involved with this evening. She bragged about drinking the Chablis with me, then he asked her what the main was.

"What's the main tonight? Rick wants to know."

"Rib-eye steaks," I answered proudly, showing her the marinating carnage. He apologized for turning her into someone with expensive tastes. Nate and Calie turned up, amused as hell by this, and she shared her crostini and Chablis with them before they kindly took off for the pub. We fucked shortly afterward between course one and two, and as we undressed and she took off her high heels, I smelled the wildest, human stink aroma of all time.

"Those are me feets," she said. "Blame my father for that."

"Wait, that's hereditary?"

"Oh yes," she affirmed, straddling me in my twin bed. I couldn't breathe, and worse, couldn't get aroused at all. You would think mine would reek, being in wet cellar boots for two months straight, but this was something I'd never encountered. Regardless, we had sex and she finished on top of me, loudly.

"I'm gonna go wash my feet now," she said. An hour later, I could smell them in the bathroom still, and Matt Wenk's repetitive quote about people and life came to me: "it takes all kinds."

I started prepping dinner, skulling the off dry Grenache Rosé. It smelled like fresh squeezed strawberry juice and tasted just as refreshing. Sweet, but at a level I could look past. Not like the sugary Kilikanoon Rosé cordial I tried up in Clare that was seriously for Grandmas if anybody. With a well-cooked dinner of carrots, thyme-cheddar mashed potatoes, and pan fried rib-eyes, Bailey and I smashed the 2001 Olive Hill in no time, which was showing crazy earthiness, rich red concentrated fruits, and a minute long finish. This was my second bottle in two weeks time. I cleared the plates and told her to relax.

Nate came home later and asked how my steaks turned out.

"Absolutely gorgeous!" she replied, offering him a glass of Draycott. "Why would I ever go to Appellation when I can have a steak like Daz made me here?"

"Hwah!" Nate replied. "Good on ya, Daz."

He could see what was coming next, finished his taste of 2004 Shiraz, and then said good night.

We headed out back so she could smoke and I could strum. She asked for some of the same songs over again. I was dizzy with gluttony but played the baritone ukulele for about twenty minutes under the gum tree beside her. There was a chill to the air, and soon Bailey finished a second cigarette and said, "Enough of that toy, Daz. I'm ready to play with something else."

CHAPTER 32

For a change of pace and some fun, I charged down south on Saturday afternoon to Knight's Beach. I booked a room at the Port Elliot Beach Hostel, which I'd eyeballed on my last trip through town. The couple running the hostel were quirky. A friendly guy that smelled of patchouli who wanted to chat about California, and a scowling, cut-to-the-chase woman who demanded payment and showed me to the accommodation. The two story building seemed old but the interiors were new, with white painted walls and no décor at all. My room was narrow with a high ceiling, street level, and had a private bath, where most of the rooms in the two story hostel had bunk beds with shared baths. Those few nights at Aaron and Steff's had given me enough of that sort of sleeping arrangement. I snacked on the Careme bakery salmon tart I'd brought down, sipped the hot, slightly volatile Kaesler 2005 Avignon GSM from a water glass, strummed, wrote, and did some night tripping around the coastal walk that was peaceful as could be. I blazed half a joint, stared up at the stars and the Gibbous moon, listened to the sea, and the phrase, "We mean nothing yet, but I mean something to you," came to mind.

* * *

I rolled up to Knight's at dawn, hearing the pounding of some set waves and feeling the chilly offshore winds. I sat on the round stone seat and watched the wave chaos ensue. The guy from the surf shop in Middleton who I'd met pulled up and watched it for a few. I'd seen his Riptide Magazine sticker on his hatchback there. He got out frothing, making some encouraging feral sounds about a couple small warped lefts that fired off from the rocks. "Out there?" I asked him. He just hooted his affirmative. I suited up and returned as he was putting on some Zinc, and paddled out cautiously. The guy from the shop was obviously a local, and was asking me about the Wedge as we floated near the cliff. We talked about bodyboarding and its dying state in California, the Mike Stewart surf movie *Fire* and how I should be going to surf the Yorke Peninsula every weekend instead of coming to Port Elliot. Whoops. Maybe next year. My board wasn't working too well for me. Maybe it was the wave. I was relieved to hear that today was the first day Knight's actually broke properly in five months. And to know that it's the only spot worth going to around here.

A teenager named Austen from outside of McLaren Vale introduced himself and talked to me between waves, sharing a bit of history of the town and where I was staying. He said bad and crazy people used to be housed at the hotel until only two years ago, and he used to walk by at night and get yelled at.

"Is it haunted?" he asked me out in the water.

"I bet it is," I said. It felt a little like a psych ward. All white walls, narrow high-ceilinged room, and lots of little rooms. He told me about the old dodgy empty house next door and how no one will buy it because of the dad and son incest that went on in there. Apparently the father used to draw or paint pictures of his illicit backwards acts and hang them on the wall. Here I thought I was in the most peaceful, quaint Oregon Coast-style town in Oz.

I surfed a bit longer then got out, exchanging info with Dylan and Austen before hitting the Port Elliot bakery. The autumn sun and offshore breeze reminded me of home. There was so much more to explore on this coastline but I was running out of South Australia time. I had a feeling I'd be back here, but not sure how or when.

* * *

I got into Gawler an hour and a half early on the way back and considered killing time at a pub. Instead, my primal urges sent me straight for Bailey's. My early arrival wasn't exactly celebrated on her part, as she opened the door with a broom in hand. After all, I looked like a soap dodger with my salted hair and skin, holy corduroys and tattered Boo Boo Records t-shirt. I believe she was nearing a place where she needed a bit of her free time back, between shuffling her kids to their dad's, working, and having these raunchy weekend rendezvouses with yours truly.

"I can totally come back in an hour or so," I offered.

"No it's okay Daz. I really just need a new vagina," she joked. She poured me a glass of Yalumba Reserve Chardonnay and went back to sweeping.

"Can I help?" I asked, putting a bottle of Riesling in her freezer to chill.

"You can help by taking a shower," she said with a smirk.

"Fair enough."

After washing up and putting on some new clothes, I came out into the kitchen to find her prepping dinner. She was determined to match Friday night's feast and had visited the butcher and fish shop in Gawler for provisions. As I rinsed lettuce and vegetables for a salad beside her in the kitchen, she tooth picked some of the fatty Angaston bacon around the cuts of beef to pan sear. We drank the bottle of Jeanneret "Big Fine Girl" Riesling that I bought at their cellar door, a winery that Philip White urged me to include in my visit to Clare. I was anxious and high for the first hour but started to relax as she put the steaks on.

We sat across from each other at the small kitchen table, drinking Olive Hill Mourvédre, and as we sliced into our steaks, the bacon wrapping wouldn't budge, and was stringy as we ate our way through it, chewing for minutes. Bailey looked concerned. "Something's off here," she said.

"Mine's good," I shrugged.

We took a few more bites and then she stood up and cleared our plates.

"I'm afraid I seared these with the plastic still on. Yep, nice work Bailey!" She removed the plastic lining between steak and bacon and recooked them a little, and though carcinogenic as hell, we finished them up savagely. I got the plates out of the way and refilled our glasses.

"So when do you finish up at Two Hands?"

"Friday," I said, taking a sip.

She brought up that I couldn't possibly get another work visa in time for next vintage at my age. But she did say that I belonged in Australia, that Australia needed me, and that she'd marry me for citizenship. Her friend had done it for two different French winemakers. Divorce in two years, don't even have to live together, just have to supply wedding photos to government agents if they turn up to investigate, have a second toothbrush in the bathroom, and some male clothing hanging in a closet. That's all.

"So come on, if you like. We'll have a big party at Burge with photos, I'll put on a white dress. But if you want me to have a baby you can find some young thing to fuck and give you one because I can't be bothered with that again."

I couldn't fathom the offer. I thought I was dreaming. I wasn't getting any hint of romanticism from her. Was her heart just walled off? Or was she smart and more mature than anyone I've ever encountered?

"So this is the last night together, eh?" she asked.

"Could be," I said.

"Bailey says hello, she doesn't say good bye."

With that, she straddled me at the table and we started making out. Soon I was stumbling hand in hand with her past the living room to her bedroom, past her ever-snoring canine on the couch.

"Bailey says hello, she doesn't say good bye," she repeated later as I drifted off to sleep.

CHAPTER 33

As a make up gesture for Ben, I brought him along as my date to Jeremy Holmes's house for dinner on Wednesday. I'd initially reached out to Jeremy, a wine importer, online, who posted regularly on wine critic Robert Parker's message board, about where I should work in Australia. My concerns at that time were not to end up at Jacob's Creek or a similar tank factory, but to make quality wine, and to pull in enough money from the gig to make it worthwhile and see some significant growth in my ability as a winemaker. He suggested Yalumba and Two Hands, and connected me with Matt Wenk.

Now that my final days in South Australia were coming to an end, Jeremy invited me to his house for dinner and wine. He happened to live next door to Nathan's house all along, at 7 A Murray, which was tucked beyond a hedge and secretive gate. Had I known this, I would've had a lot more Burgundy to write about.

Ben had never met Jeremy, but knew of the Burgundies he imported, drank, and wrote about online, and was excited. One thing I was learning about Barossa, for as small of a wine region as it is, the folks in the industry mostly stick to themselves, though gossip is akin to a daytime soap opera. Sometimes it takes a vintage casual to come all the way from America to introduce these Barossans to each other.

Ben was wearing reading glasses, a red polo shirt, dressy boots, and looking more Adelaide than Angaston. In his hands were two bottles of new age Australian wine: Michael Hall and William Downie. Finally, my bottle of Arcadian Fiddlestix Vineyard Pinot Noir was going to be shared after three months of sitting in my luggage, with most of that time being in a train car. We walked over at seven, through the gate.

"We might be attacked by dogs right now," Ben said. We knocked on the door. A tall man with short, spiky grey-black hair and a genuine smile greeted us and introduced his lovely wife, Heidi. We followed him inside to the open living and kitchen area and he poured us 2002 Jean Recaurd Champagne. We offered our bottles and he took them and lined them up on the counter, inspecting the labels.

"Ah, so you're a Downie fan, huh?" Jeremy asked Ben.

Ben blushed and said, "Not a fan, but he's making some interesting wines there."

We started snacking on a Maggie Beers paté, talking about the vintage, and getting to know each other. Looking around the house, the Holmes family had a stylish, wood-floored, modernized interior, with a chef-worthy kitchen space, art on the walls, and some toys and coloring books all about. Heidi was tending to their toddler who was just about ready for bed. The living room space boasted a view across the open lot behind their house toward the train tracks. The Tom Waits album ended and Jeremy told me to pick something out.

"Are you the guitar player," Heidi asked, having heard me on Monday out back apparently.

"Yeah," I said sheepishly.

"Lovely," she said.

I picked out Antony and the Johnsons, which at moments was too on the fringe for cocktail hour. They had lots of Leonard Cohen. We moved on to the rich, oaky 2007 Michael Hall Piccadilly Valley Chardonnay.

"So who in the Barossa do you like?" I asked the Francophile, who often posts online about the most epic and expensive of Burgundies, many of which he imports. He had opened a 1998 Chassagne Montrachet, which was being drained a lot quicker than the Piccadilly Chard. Ben looked on eagerly for his answer.

"Oh, we like Spinifex, Turkey Flat, Rockford Basket Press ages well. What the Barossa does best is Grenache, Mataro and Shiraz. It just has to be done differently now, with some restraint."

With their baby in bed, the four of us sat down for dinner and tried the herbal, almost steamed broccoli green William Downie Yarra Pinot from 2005. The wine was fermented with all of the stems intact, which can sometimes dominate the entire wine's profile.

"I'm excited to try an Arcadian," Jeremy said. "Been reading about these for awhile now."

I poured everyone a glass of it. Thankfully, the wine was incredible, with the right amount of dirtiness, wild raspberry aromatics and spice, and an everlasting finish. Jeremy's wife had a second glass, and they looked at each other, smiling, and then thanked me for flying it over. Just the path the bottle took to get here on the table was a story in itself. Ben's William Downie and the Michael Hall didn't get the same response. Jeremy put on Leonard Cohen's recent *Live in London* album and descended into his cellar, returning with a Giaconda 1999 Warner Vineyard Shiraz, and a 2007 Donnhoff Riesling with only 8.5 percent alcohol. Ben and I eagerly went in for full pours of the Giaconda, one of Australia's most iconic wineries. For being over a decade old, there was plenty of varietal Shiraz character, color, richness, and just enough tobacco and green notes to keep it alive. The Donnhoff Riesling sparked us talking about Grosset, and he stood up excitedly and said, "We won't open it tonight, but here, I'm going to give you something, but you've gotta promise to take it back to America with you. It's their oh-two Polish Hill. It'll keep for decades." Heidi disappeared to check on their little one no doubt, leaving Ben and me at the table.

"Your William Downie sucked balls," I goaded Ben, using his own kind of insult.

"It did!" he said, widening his eyes and laughing.

"It's not oh-two," Jeremy said, reemerging from the cellar, "It's two thousand five. Almost as good." He gave me the bottle as a gift, signaling our time to get going. It was close to ten o'clock.

CHAPTER 34

On my final day at Two Hands, Ben, Nathan, Calie, Heintje and I racked and blended the 2009 GSM "Brave Faces." Ben was in a good mood, cracking jokes, offering multiple espresso breaks, and even taking me to the bakery in Nuriootpa. Brave Faces was his favorite Two Hands wine and the blend came out with a little of that restraint Jeremy Holmes was talking about the Barossa Valley needing in its wines. Ben was planning on spending the weekend in Adelaide at his fiancée's parents' house, so I had a free ride into the city after work. He had me pull a five barrel composite of 2009 Aerope Grenache to taste, then I tasted through some other lots of Mataro, and the single vineyard designate Shiraz wines. It all reminded me of a breezy last day at school. Two Hands should be proud of their wines. The 2009's were all floral, juicy, elegant enough, and had soft tannins and loads of flavor, and apparently our 2010 harvest was certain to be called a "cracker" of a vintage.

I used my lunch break to format my last weekend in South Australia before flying off to New South Wales for a month of surfing. I'd decided not to stay with Ava, opting to simply catch her show on Sunday and say goodbye to keep things friendly and mellow. Emailing that news to her drew a quick, unfavorable response. I went ahead and booked the same solitary room in Glenelg Beach that I started it all off with. I replied to an email from Mick Wordley, the multi-instrumentalist and record producer who Laura had introduced me to that long-ago evening with Philip White to see if I could come record some original tunes on Saturday night.

Ben and I went over to the tank farm of Rocland near the end of the day to rack one massive tank of wine to the bottling area for the next week's bottling. As we finished up around three PM we saw Aaron, my first short term landlord, sitting in high visibility gear with three old, rugged

Rocland types on paint buckets drinking beer out of sight. They offered us Heinekens and we accepted, sitting in their circle. These guys were die hard large production wine workers, and the years dealing with massive tanks, laborious hoses that stretch for kilos, questionably large chemical and sulfite additions, and god knows what else, showed on their sunburned skins. Not much of a dental insurance policy at Rocland was the main drift I was getting. I needed subtitles for a couple of the dudes as they informed me of a nasty array of lewd sexual myths in Australia. First being the "Mahogany Canoe." "That's when you shit in a plastic bag, freeze it to bring out later and use it as a dildo on yer missus," one of the guys shared.

"How about the 'Spider Man'?" another guy asked. "You just cum in your hand and throw it at someone!"

"Ha mate, how 'bout the 'Angry Neighbor'?" Aaron offered. "Have you heard that one?"

"I can only imagine," I said.

"Angry Neighbor is when you're fucking your missus up against the front window in your living room and you step aside to let your best mate in for a go, and go outside and wave at them both through the window!"

That was a lot to take in, so we finished our beers and I said bye to Aaron. When Ben and I got in his Camry, we both looked at each other with serious eyes. "Those guys are fucking hardcore," I said.

Back at Marananga at the end of the shift, I checked my email and saw Mick Wordley's response. He invited me to a long lunch on Saturday at T-Chow in Adelaide with a wine group, and said I could head up to their house and studio afterward if I wanted. I instantly accepted. Over my time here I had written a song in the train car mostly, in the delirium of vintage, and I had a handful of others to record now that the option was presented, especially with things at an emotionally high pitch. One thing about Australia: the people make you feel like a real musician, even if you're just okay at it. In America I couldn't even get a gig at a Salt Water Taffy shop, and here I was going to record with the most respected soundman for my kind of music.

I vowed to free myself from Ava's life and lurk through my final weekend here in South Australia without being a whore, in a hostel with a bottle of Clare Valley Riesling again. My flight left on Monday morning from Adelaide to Port Macquarie, a town I knew nobody in.

Heintje awkwardly ducked out of the lab as goodbyes to Calie and me were underway. I never said goodbye to Nathan either, who also doubled as my landlord for these last two weeks. Matt locked up Marananga behind us, and I hugged him for the first time and thanked him for the experience.

On the drive to Nathan's to pack up my things and clean up, I chucked my foul cellar boots off into a vineyard near Rolf Binder's place while I drove, laughing about it. I was done. Vintage 2010 in the Southern Hemisphere was complete.

I had Ben follow me to Gawler to drop off Bailey's Mazda, in which I met her boys for the first time. She pulled me in the kitchen to make out and one of the boys watched on as the bearded American and mom tongued each other.

"This is hello," she reiterated to me.

"I'll see you again," I said, hugging her, feeling straight out of a 1950's Hollywood movie.

"You will," she affirmed. "Bailey only sells hello," she said, tearing up. "She never says goodbye."

I pulled away from her and waved at the little guys who kept coming in to have a look, then running off. She was cooking pasta for them and in the mom mode I hadn't seen before.

"Here Daz. I told Rick you'd be playing music with Mick. Open this up with him." It was a bottle of Burge Family 2007 G3: a pricey rarity from a frost-damaged year at the property.

She waved bye with one of her boys as Ben and I drove off. I was rattled a bit by her tears and this finale, and found myself shaking some. Ben broke the tension with something I'd forgotten I shared with him.

"Bailey only says hello," he teased me in a feminine whisper, merging onto the highway, looking me seriously in the eyes, "she never says goodbye."

"I've told you way too much," I said, opening a Coopers Pale Ale in the passenger seat.

We had a good drive down to the city, laughing, doing impersonations of all of our coworkers and bosses. He pointed out the flashy Two Hands office in North Adelaide as we sped past.

"No wonder they don't come up often," I said.

My only plans entailed consuming some wine, grabbing a slice of pizza, and strumming myself into a solitary sleep. We arrived outside the hostel in Glenelg.

"You've gone full circle," Ben said to me, smirking.

The hostel bar area was bustling with travelers, with house music blaring and cigarette smoke in the air. I got my room key and ordered a glass of cheap wine so I could have the glass itself to use. Once I put my things away, I walked back to that bottle shop up the street and picked out a Riesling, like a creature of habit.

CHAPTER 35

The next day I met Mick and his wife Robin at a "Less than Fifteen Dollar Bottle of Wine" themed lunch at T-Chow, a tradition founded by wine writer Philip White. Philip wasn't there, as he didn't have a driver's license and remained mostly in his shack at Yangarra. Last time I was here was during the Two Hands End of Vintage Show and I was annihilated, so it was good to see the restaurant in a steadier light. I had my luggage and the baritone uke, so I stashed it against the wall and grabbed a seat at the table. Aside from Mick and Robin and a vampire-like middle aged man, the group consisted of mainly classic wine loving older couples at the table. I brought a Skillogallee Gewürztraminer which got the nod for top white of the luncheon. The Spinifex Papillon was the red wine of the day, brought by an American ex-pat living and farming Sauvignon Blanc in New Zealand. I talked to the overweight man next to me with a bloated nose about how I went to Penfolds and they didn't pour me any Grange.

"Aw mate," he said, "you're not missing anything. Henschke Mount Edelstone Shiraz is Australia's greatest red wine, above Grange or Hill of Grace easy!"

"I've had that once and it was the 1990," I affirmed. "Phenomenal."

The sentiment was seconded with a nod by the quiet and mysterious man next to him.

Afterward, Mick and Robin drove me up into their hilly, spacious, tree-lined neighborhood. They had a two story house and I set my things in the doorway. A parrot shrieked from its cage in the living room, next to a wall of records and discs. Mick washed his hands in the sink and then started hand mixing some fermenting dough in a bowl as I stood by and asked him about the house, his recording studio, shows he'd been to. But our attention went to the dough again, and he shared how he uses a starter that is decades old from a chef at the Hilton in Sydney. Mick kept it alive daily in a large glass jar. I'd never seen anything like it before.

"I'll send you home with a jar of it, if you promise to keep it alive. Or promise to get it through customs!"

I talked about my family's pizzeria and how we'd always used yeast packets. The conversation then turned to wild yeast versus commercial yeast and how to keep a starter alive. He formed a loaf right there and turned on his oven.

An hour later, while snacking on warm bread, olives and cheese and having some wine, Mick's indoor parrot kept flapping at me and landing on my head, its claws moving into my scalp. It was funny at first, but I must've looked unnerved the fourth or fifth time it happened. He finally put it away and told it, "Stop that." During dinner we heard this raspy phrase coming from the cage. It'd chirp and then whisper "stop that" in Mick's exact voice, over and over again. "Stop that. Raaa! Chirp. Stop that."

We retreated with our glasses and the bottle of Burge Family G3 to the lair and attached wing of the house, dubbed Mixmasters Studio. Mick opened up a few guitar cases and showed me options of what I could play. There was a beautiful old Gibson acoustic that got my attention. I opened the G3 and carefully poured some into our glasses. Before I knew it, I was in the recording area behind the glass wall. I played my heart out, recording fifteen songs, half original and half covers. I kept checking back in with Mick to see if what was coming out was okay, or if enough was enough, but he encouraged me to keep going. Five hours later my voice was shot and Mick was done. I sat with him at the control board as he played back one of the tracks.

"I messed up the lyrics there," I said about the Bob Dylan tune "It's All Over Now, Baby Blue." "I did the last verse first."

"It's not messin' it up mate. Dylan does it on purpose now, so it's right."

He was nice enough to load all the tracks on a disc right there, and he wrote *Darren Delmore, Adelaide* on the disc. He handed it to me.

"If you decide to do anything with any of this, just let me know in advance."

Mick showed me the small bedroom next to the studio itself, with a vintage espresso machine in there and sink. "Sleep well," he said.

CHAPTER 36

I turned up at Ava's place around noon the next day, feeling more like an actual musician than I ever would again. I decided to stop by before the gig to say goodbye privately, and pay her the $160 I owed her for auto repairs. I knocked, feeling nervous, but she didn't answer, so I walked up Melbourne Street and called her from a pay phone. She picked up. Her voice was trashed. She said she had to cancel her gig at the Wheatsheaf today, and that she felt terrible about it.

"I'm right around the corner," I said.

"Aw I'm half naked. Give me some time." My dollar coin ran out before I could say I would. I browsed through the wines at Melbourne Street Wine Cellars then went over. She was in a white fluffy skirt over black stockings with her hair wet. Her face was puffy and her eyes red and glazed.

"To be honest I wasn't expecting you today," she said. "I sent you heaps of messages about my voice and..." There were stacks of rubber banded guest checks all over the floor of her living room. "Excuse the mess. I'm doing my taxes. I have to run errands. We ran out of stuff at the shop. I have things to do."

"Oh okay, well do you wanna just do a quick coffee or?"

"Yeah, that'll do. Let me go dry my hair."

I sat on her couch, feeling this heavy, guilty sensation. It would have been easier to have not come here, to just walk away. I wasn't sure what I was even trying to achieve. It's not like I was going to confess to my simultaneous rendezvous with Bailey. What good would that do? Did I want to feel better about myself? My last real relationship lasted a total of nine months just before I came on this adventure. I didn't mean to hurt Ava, and it couldn't have been more obvious that I had.

I pulled out the money and put it on the table. She came back downstairs with her skirt accidentally tucked into her stockings in the back, flying around the room with erratic energy. I was going to have to tell her that her ass was exposed, but luckily she did one last mirror check and gasped at the sight of it and sorted things out. We walked to Cibo and she handed me a five dollar bill for a soy cappuccino.

"Nah I got this," I said, refusing it.

"You take it," she said sternly.

I ordered the drinks from a cheery counter girl and I carried them out to the patio. We talked about her voice, the cancelled gig, how I should've come down to Laura's bonfire on Friday night, where I was going. She made a joke about Port Macquarie being the lamest town in Australia, full of squares and geezers. She could barely look at me, even with her large dark sunglasses on. I tried to keep things upbeat, which probably made me look like I was just along for the ride.

We walked back to her place, and I thought we were just going in so I could get my things but she opened her car doors and said, "Get in." She took me on her errand run, I pushed her shopping cart, stood by her side at check out, and carried in all the ice cream cartons and strawberries into her shop. Seeing Cosecha in the day time was like a strip club seen through sober eyes. That dark, red light allure that made it such a romantic place to spend a late evening looked like any closed, crumb filled restaurant in the daytime.

Back at her house, I reached for my backpack and said, "Well I should get out of your space." I held my luggage and baritone ukulele.

"Well, where are you going?" she asked, looking at me in the entryway.

"The Wheaty. I'll grab a taxi."

"Ah! I'll take you. Come on."

"You don't have to do that."

"No, come on, but take that pack off and give me a proper hug now."

I held her for minutes there, in the ground floor of her flat, and apologized for making her cry, told her how much I enjoyed her company, and that I was going to miss her.

"You didn't make me cry," she clarified, pulling away and denying it.

The drive over was mostly quiet and intense. She dropped me in the rear parking lot of the Wheatsheaf Hotel, and gave me a long passionate hug on the street that wetted my eyes.

"You can take my gig," she said. "Just tell Robyn you want it."

"Nah, it's your gig, Ava."

"When I come to California you better show me some hospitality!" she said, pushing on my chest.

She drove away, leaving me with my uke, hat, and bags at the Wheatsheaf Hotel. I felt relieved as she disappeared down the street. Inside the Wheatsheaf bar area, I ordered a pint and sat at a table with my stuff all around me, journaling things down. The Yearlings arrived to set up and I said hello, but they didn't recognize me from a few months beforehand. I watched them play half of their set, then took a taxi to Glenelg Beach, checked back into the hostel, and bought a cold bottle of KT Riesling from Clare Valley to drink on the balcony. The beach town was quiet for a change, being a Sunday. At night I took a walk around the empty beach, smoked my last joint, laid back in the sand and stared up into the night sky.

CHAPTER 37

A depression of sorts seems to settle in after any good trip to foreign lands, and especially after the climax of being a part of a weighty wine harvest with its ups and downs, colored by characters both good and not so great, and moments that make you laugh or break you down. It's a bubble that you thrash inside for an insane amount of hours, adhering to its boundaries, crammed in with these people from all over the globe, sweating and working collectively harder than you ever had before, when it suddenly bursts open and it's over in a splash. Once everything's been turned to wine and poured into barrels for the winter, with grape leaves crinkling and blowing in the colder autumn winds, there's not much left for a temporary cellar hand to do then be "headin' for another joint," as Bob Dylan sang on "Tangled up in Blue." Maybe "tangled" is a more appropriate feeling than "depressed." All you can do is move on to another stint or, more darkly looming off in the distance, a real job filled with real obligations.

The trouble with memories for me is that it's impossible to make the good ones last, and to be able to revive them on cue like a film reel in my mind. My vices certainly didn't do much for clarity. However, the worst memories tend to be immortal, frustratingly so. Which is why I wrote as much down about my life at Two Hands Wines and in the lucky country as physically possible, before the images, the slang, the laughter and the "love" left me forever. For better or for worse, this four-month stage of my life would live on, safely in pages and as they really happened, at least for me.

On the fourteen hour long Qantas flight from Sydney to Los Angeles I couldn't sleep to save my life, no matter how many 187 ml bottles of Pikes Clare Valley Riesling the flight attendant served me. I filled the pages of my journal until my hands cramped up, worked out the crazed mathematics of my remaining income and how it would hopefully get me through June and July with intermittent shifts at my family's pizzeria, before shoving off to the redwood studded Anderson Valley in August to another new winemaking adventure and human "social experiment," as Michael Twelftree kept referring to all of us working vintage at Two Hands.

Speaking of Twelftree, he and Matt Wenk invited me back for the next vintage and even offered to make me a manager so the airfare would be covered with some increased pay. I accepted the offer mid-way through my month long surf trip in New South Wales. In a way, on the scribbled pages of my journal while sitting in my airline seat, I'd mapped out another full year of my life as a vagabond cellarhand, and the show would go on. It was easy to want this forever, all this drifting and dreaming. Why wouldn't you?

And with that all seemingly sorted, I reclined as much as I could, put on my headphones and clicked on Kris Kristofferson's *The Silver Tongued Devil and I* album, then lowered my Qantas sleep mask over my eyes and finally fell asleep at 38,000 feet.

LUCKY COUNTRY

Confessions of a Vagabond Cellarhand